The Presence

A Memoir of Miracles

First published by O Books, 2010
O Books is an imprint of John Hunt Publishing Ltd., The Bothy, Deershot Lodge, Park Lane, Ropley,
Hants, SO24 0BE, UK
office1@o-books.net
www.o-books.net

Distribution in:

UK and Europe
Orca Book Services
orders@orcabookservices.co.uk
Tel: 01202 665432 Fax: 01202 666219
Int. code (44)

USA and Canada
NBN
custserv@nbnbooks.com
Tel: 1 800 462 6420 Fax: 1 800 338 4550

Australia and New Zealand
Brumby Books
sales@brumbybooks.com.au
Tel: 61 3 9761 5535 Fax: 61 3 9761 7095

Far East (offices in Singapore, Thailand,
Hong Kong, Taiwan)
Pansing Distribution Pte Ltd
kemal@pansing.com
Tel: 65 6319 9939 Fax: 65 6462 5761

South Africa
Alternative Books
altbook@peterhyde.co.za
Tel: 021 555 4027 Fax: 021 447 1430

Text copyright Robert Page 2008

Design: Stuart Davies

ISBN: 978 1 84694 268 6

A CIP catalogue record for this book is available
from the British Library.

Printed by Digital Book Print

The Presence

A Memoir of Miracles

Robert Page

BOOKS

Winchester, UK
Washington, USA

CONTENTS

For my wife, Joan Kurn.

"The truest end of life is to
know the life that never ends."
William Penn

"... The man who can articulate the movements of his inner life,
who can give names to his varied experiences, need no longer
be a victim of himself, but is able slowly and consistently to
remove the obstacles that prevent the spirit from entering. He is
able to create space for Him whose heart is greater than his,
whose eyes see more than his, and whose hands can heal more
than his."
Henri J Nouwen The Wounded Healer

Preface

I always think of myself as a pretty Ordinary Joe who happens to have lived a somewhat less than conventional life which, in one important part, can be fairly described as a lifestyle not to be emulated. Although I have a relaxed approach to many issues there are two I believe we ignore at our peril. While the one remains largely in the background both inform almost everything I write in *The Presence*.

There is, first, the number of lives we allow to be unfulfilled. It distresses me more than I can possibly say to witness so many youngsters with so much potential wasting their lives rather than directing their energies to more satisfying and useful ends. There are then the older people who start to wonder where they have gone wrong after becoming painfully aware of having achieved so much less than their capabilities made possible.

Second, and even more important, because it is so often at the root of failure and disillusion, is what I see as the general lack of recognition of the spiritual dimension at the heart of our being. I believe passionately that those who would enjoy the infinitely wonderful gift of life to the full need to nurture this dimension with even more care than they give to their minds and bodies.

The Presence is a deeply personal book designed to draw its readers into the intimacies I share with them. It is, in one respect, a memoir of experiences I can only regard as miraculous, the most remarkable of these being the conversion experience I describe early in the Prologue. It is also an account of my continuing journey towards, eventually, something approaching spiritual maturity.

My alcoholism and a recovery of somewhat more than 30 years are factors I cannot, and do not, ignore. They are, in truth, the source of whatever authority I may fairly claim in speaking with you. Even so, I hope I have nowhere allowed my alcoholism to overshadow the importance of the lessons I have learned and absorbed since being freed of the shackles of addiction. These have meaning for everyone, whatever their condition or station in life. In especial case, I hope they may have meaning for you, whatever your condition or station in life.

I address subjects to which I have been obliged to give particular attention in developing my present relationship with God. These provide the main, but by no means the only, themes of *The Presence*. The most prominent of the subjects I discuss are:

Plain speaking and the acceptance of personal responsibility;

The many unrecognized encounters we have with God and His sometimes surprising agents of personal development;

What it is to be "born again";

Why we need to do more than to eliminate what is undesirable from our speech and actions... The story of the three little pigs;

How and why we must embrace a policy of rigorous self-honesty if we are to progress in our spiritual lives (an argument which includes an example from life);

The reality of the unconditional love offered by God;

Why we can do no other than to love God, Christ and our neighbor exactly - *exactly!* - as we love ourselves (with another example from life);

Social conditioning and "the sins of the fathers" and how "the sins of the fathers" can lead not to punishment visited upon the children, grandchildren and great-grandchildren of the father, but to understanding, forgiveness, love, healing and freedom; and

A further look at our encounters with God and His agents, and how we must "die" if we would live.

*

I should like to thank Ken Buggy, my spiritual director, for making this book possible.   RP

Prologue

Picture if you will the scene in the Garden at Gethsemane on the night of Jesus' arrest. The time of his ordeal on the cross was drawing near. Eleven of his disciples were with him. Judas Iscariot was the absentee.

Then, according to John's Gospel (18.1-11), "Judas came to the grove, guiding a detachment of soldiers and some officials from the chief priests and Pharisees. They were carrying torches, lanterns and weapons."

I wonder how Judas and his party expected to be met. With lies? With accusations of treachery? By flight or fight? By fear? By anger? We will never know. Whatever the case, according to John they were so surprised by Jesus' response that "they drew back and fell to the ground".

All Jesus did was to go out and meet them.

"Who is it you want?" he asked.

"Jesus of Nazareth."

Knowing exactly what was in their minds Jesus gave an answer which is a classic in simplicity. "I am he."

No surly, "Who wants to know?"

No aggressive, "What do you want him for?"

No indignant, "Don't you know what time it is?"

No evasive, "I'll go and see if he's here."

No prevarication of any kind.

Just a simple, "I am he."

Such is the way of the world, for some things never change, even this was not enough. Jesus had to repeat both his question and his answer before the arresting party believed he was who he said he was.

Fascinating though that exchange is it was only a small part of the unfolding drama, but a part by no means overshadowed by later events.

Why not?

Because Jesus, in the direst circumstances, said simply, "I am he."

I hope you will find such directness and simplicity written into every page of this little book which is, above all, a celebration of the power of God to transform lives. It is, quite literally, a memoir of miracles.

(2)

Until the space age dawned it was held that whatever goes up must come down. With the exception of space probes this is still true. I believe there is a similar spiritual law: what goes into a person must at some time come out, in one form or another. It has most certainly been a truth of my life and so, although I did not find it easy to commit to paper my deepest and most intimate thoughts, feelings and beliefs; or to give an account of the experiences which have most profoundly affected me, these are the things I have tried most openly to share with you. I hope this sharing will do you as much good as it has done me, for I have found that the reverse of the spiritual law I stated above is also true: what comes out of a person must at some time return, in one form or another.

"Give, and it will be given to you. A good measure, pressed down, shaken together and running over, will be poured into your lap. For with the measure you use, it will be measured to you" (Luke 6.38).

Most of all I hope that what I share with you speaks less of me, much less, than it does of him to whom my thanks and all credit are due: Jesus Christ.

(3)

There is no better place for me to begin than my own very

personal Calvary. Everything I share with you in the following pages revolves around this pivotal moment. It came about on the morning of Saturday, 23 April 1977, after 20 hours or so of pure horror.

On the previous day I had taken my first drink late in the morning. I continued drinking in the Victoria bus station in Nottingham until my cash was very nearly all gone. It was a strange day because, however much I drank - and it was a lot - I just could not get properly drunk. By this I mean I remained aware of what was happening around me.

For a reason I cannot remember, at some time in the afternoon I forced my way into the home I had shared with my wife and children until two months earlier. I have vague memories of literally fighting with my wife and oldest daughter and of tearing the telephone from the wall, but that is all.

A little later an ambulance overtook me as I lurched along a nearby road. It stopped and the ambulance men got out and correctly identified me. They wanted me to go to hospital with them. I refused. They drove away.

From there I somehow made my way to my parents' flat and begged them to give me a bed for the night. Bless them, they did.

My memories of that night are vague, nightmarish and, quite possibly, inaccurate. I will recall them as best I can. I remember experiencing fear such as I had never before known; I remember sweating and shaking; and I remember the many thousands of hallucinatory spiders that crawled all over me and the bed on which I lay. The wretched creatures changed the color of the walls of the room from Magnolia to a seething black. I have no memory of either my mother or father looking in on me but, apparently, they did: many times.

I must have slept because I can remember waking up and craving alcohol. Worse, and it was absolute madness, I was in a mood to do anything in order to get it, even to steal by violence from my parents who, at the time, were 84 and 74 years old.

I more or less fell off the bed and staggered to the door. When I opened it there, on its other side, with a hand outstretched towards the handle, stood my mother. For a second or two - it might have been somewhat longer - neither of us moved. We simply stood and looked at one another.

It is here that my memory becomes startlingly clear.

Even as I write I can see vividly the tiredness and distress on my mother's face and the shaking in her hands. Despite this I felt no emotion whatsoever: neither sadness to see her in such a state, nor remorse that I should be the one responsible for her condition, or of anything else even half human. All I cared about was laying my hands on the money that would buy my next drunk.

Then, and God alone knows why I did it, I reached out and took my mother's hands as she reached for mine. This in itself was radical stuff. We were not a hand-holding, hugging or kissing kind of family.

Even more astonishingly I suddenly blurted out, "I need help."

That was another first. I had never, ever, before asked anyone for help in anything more significant than the trivial, and then only rarely. Now I did and now I meant it. No sooner had the words tottered from my tongue than I was drenched in peace and love. They seemed to enter the top of my head and pass through my body, all the way down to my feet, as though they were liquids poured from a bucket. Everything; all movement, every motion of my mind, stopped in that most exquisitely beautiful of moments. There was no before, no after; time had ceased to exist. All was distilled in the clarity of that stillness. This was not all. In that doorway, sharing the space with my mother and me, I sensed a living and vital Presence. This Presence was, in the splendor of its invisible reality, the Love and the Peace I was experiencing. It held me in its arms; it surrounded me, and it was in me; it was not of me, and yet it was one with me, a part of me. This is nonsense language I know, but I cannot better describe those wonderful, miraculous, healing moments.

Then the Presence was no more. It was gone. Gone too was the distress and the tiredness in my mother's face; gone was my craving for alcohol. Rather than suffering craving I rejoiced in the sure knowledge that I need never drink again: need never, not would never.

Some time later I gave to that Divine Presence the name of Jesus. Today, 30 and more years after the event, I think of it rather as the Holy Spirit.

It has been put to me that what happened on that morning was no more than the manifestation of a sudden and profound psychological change. That I did undergo a sudden and profound psychological change is beyond question, but it was a change brought about, I believe, by a Light. That Light was the same Light that so brilliantly illuminated Jesus' life on earth. I thank God that it shone on mine, however briefly.

Those few moments I shared with my mother - and her experience of them mirrored mine - are moments in which a dead man saw the face of God, died, and was reborn into a life far, far, richer than any he had dreamed possible.

(4)

When he spoke in the synagogue at Nazareth at the very start of his ministry Jesus began by telling his listeners, in language which falls uneasily on the modern western ear, that the Spirit of the Lord was on him. This same Spirit, he said, had anointed him "to preach good news to the poor... to proclaim freedom for the prisoners and recovery of sight for the blind, to release the oppressed" (Luke 4.18).

That is exactly what he did for the Bob Page who died and was then reborn. The man who died was most certainly afflicted. He was held in thrall to alcohol, in a prison built with bricks shaped from the clays of oppression: fear, resentment, bitterness, delusion, loneliness and a paralyzing sense of his own inadequacy and worthlessness. He could see no way forward, no hope of anything better, nothing but darkness and emptiness.

This man was beaten and crushed, so he had to die. He had to die in order that he might live. Die he did. Fortunately, at the moment of his death that man recognized his plight and uttered the most heartfelt prayer of his life: "I need help."

What else were those three words if not a prayer of the heart?

God, as the Holy Spirit, came to that benighted man who, though he breathed, was dead.

God came and by breathing his life into him gave to this newly born, newly free man the eyes and the vision to see that he did have a life to live, as a man, free from the oppression of alcohol.

Life. It's a wonderful word, isn't it? Life, the opposite of death. And it had been given to me. Wonderful!

That was the good news. It would have been better had I known how to live this life. But I didn't, and it wasn't long before I began to appreciate just how great was my ignorance. Thank God I took the opportunity offered to me and spent the first ten weeks of my recovery in the local addiction unit. This created a very necessary breathing space in which I could start to wonder how I might best approach my new life. One of my better ideas was to begin to attend meetings of Alcoholics Anonymous whilst I was still a patient in the addiction unit. I had flirted with AA before but, being unwilling to learn, I learned precisely nothing. Surprise, surprise!

Strangely, and many years were to pass before I began to understand why, no sooner had I put the bottle down than I found myself with a positive craving for quality reading. I read everything of worth I could lay my hands on, including, to my great surprise, poetry. The only previous experience I had had of poetry was during a few chaotic months in late adolescence, but that is another story. Alongside this craving for literature I experienced an equal longing to immerse myself in music. My spiritual appetites were beginning to surface and to demand long overdue satisfaction.

This was all very positive but, at the same time, those same weeks were weeks of great confusion and uncertainty. Perhaps the only thing of real significance I learned in their passing was that I had been, and still was, a very sick man. I had great difficulty in accepting that it would take me as long as two or three years even remotely to approach what is known as "normality".

For the ten weeks I remained in the addiction unit and for a long time afterwards I dug deeply into the gospels in further response to the demands of my spiritual appetite. I gained a great deal from those passages in which Jesus' spoken ministry is quoted. These and the post-resurrection stories I read time and time again. The attraction of the post-resurrection stories is not difficult to understand: the link between them and the new life I had been given is pretty transparent.

The vital point I wish to make here - it cannot be over-emphasized - is the tremendous impact made on me by so many of Jesus' words. (Without knowing it I was practicing *lectio divina*.) Very often it seemed almost as though Jesus himself rose up from the printed page and spoke to me:

"I am the resurrection and the life. He who believes in me will live, even though he dies..." (John 11.25).

"I am the Way; I am Truth and Life..." (John14.6 NJB).

"Peace I leave with you; my peace I give you. I do not give to you as the world gives. Do not let your hearts be troubled and do not be afraid" (John 14.27).

At this early stage in my recovery, which always has been a spiritual adventure, I understood only a small part of the passages such as those I have quoted above. The few openings I was given were rarely ones I could then express in words. This mattered not at all. Their gentle, benevolent, influence on me was, and remains, something beyond price.

Other than being enabled to stay clear of the bottle my greatest gain was a wonderful sense of hope. And it was wonderful; so, so, wonderful; nothing short of miraculous. Darkness? Emptiness? Despair? They never stood a chance before the Light of the Hope that is Jesus Christ.

That hope has not been disappointed.

It has been exceeded.

I rejoice that the insights given to me in those early days have since been expanded. Now I am able to express many of them in words. Interestingly, nothing I have since learned has opposed any of those early insights; nor have any of them led me adrift. The simple truth is that they became essential parts of my being and of my every striving. They remain so to this day, as I remain a very flawed human being.

(5)

One passage from the early days of my gospel reading stands out head and shoulders above the rest, for the very simple reason that it is the one from which I gained most, and - rarity of rarities - in a way I could put into words. Time has not diluted by one jot my enjoyment of reading and living this passage which, for me, is possibly the most meaningful of the post-resurrection stories.

I did not appreciate at the time how analogous my new life was to a journey of exploration. I stood at its start looking along an unknown road leading to goodness knows where. This was no doubt why I identified so readily with two other travelers walking along another road at another time. They were probably as confused as me.

Towards the very end of his gospel (24.13-35) Luke tells the story of two of Jesus' followers, Cleopas and an unnamed friend - I shall call him Jacob - walking along the road from Jerusalem to Emmaus some hours after Jesus' tomb had been found to be empty.

They were discussing all that had happened over the past few days. Who can blame them if they didn't know what to make of it? Who can blame them if they were fearful and uncertain, not knowing where to go or what to do next? No doubt they looked at each other in vain for support and reassurance.

The risen Jesus joined them but, in the words of the gospel, "they were kept from recognizing him".

Jesus asked the two what they were talking about. At this the travelers stopped, looking sad, and Cleopas expressed surprise that the stranger did not know of the things that had happened. He went on to talk of Jesus of Nazareth, whom he described as powerful in word and deed before God and all the people. He spoke of the trial and crucifixion, and the hopes he had placed on Jesus as the Redeemer of Israel. Finally, he broke the startling news of the empty tomb, discovered only that morning.

Far from being in any way surprised by what he heard the stranger rebuked the two for being slow to believe all that the prophets had said. He then went through the scriptures and explained everything the prophets had foretold about himself, from Moses on.

Cleopas and Jacob were enthralled by what they heard. Though they still did not recognize who it was that spoke to them in such a way, they did recognize Truth. So, when they reached Emmaus late in the day, they invited Truth to stay with them. Let me repeat that one: though Cleopas and Jacob did not recognize who it was that spoke it they did recognize Truth, and they invited it in.

Having been invited in Jesus stayed with the two friends.

Truth never refuses an invitation.

At table Jesus took the bread, gave thanks, broke it, and handed it round. The guest had become the host.

Whenever and wherever Truth is welcome it takes over; not as a monstrous tyrant but as a loving guide to freedom.

It was then that Cleopas' and Jacob's eyes were opened and they recognized who it was they were entertaining. In that moment Jesus disappeared from their sight.

But his truth remained.

(6)

Although my understanding of the story of Cleopas and Jacob was the first I was able to express in words it did not come quickly. My slowness had its origins in skepticism: attractive though they were I doubted the literal truth of the post-resurrection stories related in the gospels. To make matters worse, if they did not represent the literal truth I could see no value in them other than as spiritual fairy tales. It never occurred to me that their greatest meaning and worth might be found in looking on them in the revealing light of myth and metaphor.

The point I am trying to make is that we can read the story of Jesus appearing to Cleopas and Jacob on the road to Emmaus without it having the slightest impact on our own lives. There is nothing in it that directly affects us and changes what we all know. Or is there?

My skepticism was challenged one evening as I lay in bed reading a novel. I was concentrated on it; it was the only thing in my mind. Neither Jesus, nor Emmaus, nor Cleopas and Jacob were anywhere in my conscious thoughts. Until, that is, my reading was brought to a sudden halt as, again, I was saturated in love and peace and freed from all sense of time. It was an experience remarkably similar to that of 23 April 1977.

The story of Cleopas and Jacob walking the road to Emmaus became very real to me in that moment. I might have been on the road with them.

Here I find myself in some difficulty. In the event the new reality of the story presented itself to me as a complete package. It had no beginning, no middle and no end. It just was. Although

I can express my understanding of that reality in words, I was, and am, also aware of a further understanding that is beyond words, an understanding for which there are no words. This was true then; it is true now, more than thirty years on.

Now, as then, all I have with which to express the reality of the truths opened to me are words and my life. The story of the two travelers on the road to Emmaus is, for me, no longer simply a story but a signpost on the road to my understanding of the Jesus who walks with me.

It is a walk filled with wonder because there is, in truth, no road, no Emmaus, no destination of any kind, no map or chart. All I have is myself and a story. The story is the story of the man Jesus; a man born of woman, a man who grew up in a small town and who learned a trade; a man who walked and talked, ate and slept, just like you and me. He knew love and he knew anger; he knew joy and he knew sadness; he knew peace and he knew conflict. His whole story is that of a man who knew life in all its fullness. What separates him from me is his absolute faith in his Father and his obedience to Him. Jesus bowed himself to the will of his Father regardless of the cost. As yet I have found neither the faith nor the courage to follow his example. Mountains stand unmoved before me.

There is purpose in me laboring Jesus' humanity: it enables me to identify with him. The identification matters. It matters to me very much that Jesus shared many of his daily routines with me, you and everyone else. It matters to me that he had to eat, sleep and to go through all the routines of daily living. I can love and worship such a man because he did it all, and more, so superbly well. The guidance he gives me is the guidance of a man who knows from his own experience what it is I feel in whatever circumstance I may find myself. Jesus knows all about my doubts, my fears, my failings, my stupidities and everything else that makes me tick. Because he knows he does not condemn. Instead he loves me with the love of a man who has walked the same road as me and who positively wants to walk it time and time and time again - with me, with you, with anyone who wants to find meaning in their life.

This Jesus is not a remote other-worldly figure but, if you'll excuse the use of a horrible expression currently in vogue, an accessible one. He is the man Cleopas and Jacob invited to dine with them. Can you not picture that quite beautiful moment when the two travelers issued their invitation to Jesus? Truth had presented itself and drawn a welcoming response. But this was not enough. Truth will not impose itself; it needs a positive invitation. We are speaking here of love, not tyranny.

So, what happened and how did it happen? As the trio approached Emmaus, Truth, so Luke tells us, "acted as if he were going further. But they (Cleopas and Jacob) urged him strongly, 'Stay with us, for it is nearly evening.'"

Once it had been made welcome and invited in Truth became the person of Jesus. A little later, after he revealed himself, he disappeared from the sight of his guests. One glimpse of the truth of Jesus, one split second of revelation, one fleeting kiss of the Spirit, and a life is changed. The direction, purpose and meaning of that life can never, ever, be the same again. This I firmly believe. It was true on the road to Emmaus; it is true now. Nor is it some vague, impersonal, philosophical truth, interesting but, in the final analysis, neither here nor there. It is the truth of experience; a priceless, life changing truth that applies to me as much is it applied to Cleopas and Jacob; and as much to you as to me.

It is a magnificent truth.

As Luke approaches the end of this part of his gospel he says that, after Jesus had disappeared from their sight, Cleopas and Jacob were of one mind in saying, "Were not our hearts burning within us while he talked with us on the road and opened the scriptures to us?"

Of course their hearts burned within them. They were

hearing, recognizing and absorbing truth spoken with love. That love transformed the scriptures they knew so well. Dead words became a living experience; the old became new. Knowledge faded into insignificance in the light of understanding.

What was true for Cleopas and Jacob became true for me that evening as I lay in bed with my book. I had learned that Jesus can, and does, speak through anyone and anything; in any and all circumstances; at any time; in any place. I did not, however, hear his most persuasive voice until some time later when I managed finally to cast off the shackles that bound me to the literal truth and began to value more highly, as Jesus does, the metaphor, symbol and parable. I am glad I did for otherwise I should not have been able to harvest anything of the truths and the wisdom contained in works such as the Upanishads, the Bhagavad-Gita and the Dhammapada.

In this way I started in earnest to acquire a small measure of skill in the hitherto baffling art of living. My starting point was, in a very real sense, Emmaus; for it was from there I set out on the adventure that is my journey with only my alcoholism, the total of my life and the story of a man, Jesus. Join me. Please.

Chapter 1

Nothing has ever had a more profound and far-reaching effect on me than my experience of the Divine Presence on the morning of 23 April 1977, that happiest of St. George's days. After that it was impossible for anything ever to be the same again, for which I thank God from the bottom of my heart.

It is by no means stretching the truth for me to say I was born into a new life, or born again or, even, born from above.

Frankly, "born again" is not an expression I like. It reminds me too strongly of some of the more painful encounters I had with religion as a child at Sunday school. I prefer "born from above", not simply because it is free from any negative personal association, but because I feel it describes more clearly a truly remarkable happening.

My understanding of what it is to be "born from above" is based root and branch in the experience itself. The same experience gives me an equally clear understanding of what does not fall under this heading.

Let me first get the negative out of the way and at the same time lay the ghost of those wretched Sunday school encounters. I was told by several well meaning teachers that if I was truly sorry for all the wrongs I had done Jesus would forgive me. All I had to do was open my heart and invite him in. When he entered, as he surely would, I should be saved; it would be as if I had been "born again".

Although I still counted my birthdays in single figures and had probably not committed too many mortal sins, the idea of being saved terrified me. I had this truly awful vision of becoming the saintly little monster my mother wanted me to be. Little Lord Fauntleroy would have been the devil incarnate when compared with that poor wretch. There was, of course, the equally hideous possibility of going around for the rest of my life smelling of mothballs, like the elderly men who taught me. Ugh!

Neither saintliness nor mothballs were for me. In the whole of my young life I had never been more certain of anything. To be saved, to be born again, was to be freed from sin, to be permanently good, when what I wanted more than anything was to commit a few wholesome sins. Getting dirty would have been great for starters; a few acts of blatant disobedience would have been better still.

Wishful thinking. It never happened.

Now that I have had the experience of being "born from above" I know full well that I do not enjoy divine exemption from the proclivity to do wrong or not to do what is right. Being "born from above" - and this is a point I cannot emphasize too strongly - was far more exciting than this. I was given the opportunity to embark on the adventure of a completely new life.

Opportunity.

Note the word.

Most of us have probably said at some time or other, "If only I could have my time again, knowing what I know now." In many respects being born from above is remarkably similar to having that wish granted. There is a snag. The process of learning what I knew before I was given the opportunity to start on a new life had played a very large part in shaping the personality and character of the man I became.

This was awkward.

The man I became had wreaked havoc wherever he went and very nearly killed himself into the bargain. This was not how I wanted to be for the rest of my life.

When I finally absorbed this truth I was obliged to accept the further truth that there must have been a lot wrong in what I learned. From this arose the dreadful possibility that I might not be capable of learning better. Had I not over many years repeated the same mistakes time and time and time again, regardless of the quite unnecessary trouble and pain they had caused just about everyone with whom I came into contact? Why, for goodness sake? Why? I was an intelligent man. Why had I not been able to see the suffering I caused?

(2)

I need not have worried. What this relentless self-questioning meant was simply that, having got over the euphoria of realizing that a life without alcohol was possible, I had begun unwittingly to search for the roots of my alcoholism. Had I not undertaken this I am inclined to believe that whilst I might, just might, have been able not to drink again, my spiritual life would have suffered greatly. Spiritual growth and recovery from alcoholism are synonymous.

I began to look not only at the many mistakes I made but how I came to make them. It soon became horrifyingly apparent how little I thought out my responses to everyday situations. The thoughtful response was a rarity; the reaction as by reflex was all too often my way.

A little more time was to pass before I began to appreciate how rare it was for me ever to have taken the initiative in anything, especially in the direction and ordering of my own life. I had lived a life of reaction, not action.

Again I had to ask myself why this should have been; why, in truth, it still was. In addition to being intelligent, could I not also lay fair claim to being capable and imaginative?

(3)

Questions by the score began to race round my head, but they could all be distilled in the one: why am I the man I am? It was an important question. I didn't like myself.

Among my many shortcomings I particularly disliked

(a) almost always seeking to give what I believed to be

acceptable answers to questions I was asked, rather than truthful ones;

(b) habitually bending the truth to cast a more favorable light on my actions;

(c) dramatizing mundane incidents to make my life sound as exciting as I believed other peoples' to be; and

(d) spending a high proportion of my otherwise unoccupied time in a world of fantasy (frequently involving a romantic interlude with an incredibly beautiful, intelligent and sensual woman).

What all of this ridiculous way of thinking and behaving amounted to was that I was desperately afraid of "finding myself". Why? Because, beneath the image of confidence I tried so hard and so unsuccessfully to project I was convinced I was nothing but a boring, worthless, nonentity; an utter nobody with nothing to offer.

I had so poor an opinion of myself that when I listened to the stories of other members of Alcoholics Anonymous I decided I wasn't even a half decent alcoholic. I hadn't, for instance, captained a cargo ship under the influence of drink and rammed a tug-boat; I hadn't tried to land a Tiger Moth on Malta and missed the island as well as the runway; I hadn't been a showbiz celebrity notorious for my womanizing, worst luck; I hadn't been a high earner in industry; I couldn't even say I'd done time, or drunk methylated spirits, or sat around in drinking "schools", or any of the truly alcoholic things everyone else seemed to have done. Even my drinking career had been boring.

While all of this soul-searching might appear to be pretty negative it was, in truth, a considerable step forward. For the first time in my life I had begun seriously to question my ways of thinking and behaving without resort to alcohol. I knew, too, that I would not, could not, be satisfied until I found answers that made a better life possible. It hardly mattered that the answers I found might not be immediately palatable. For instance, some of the views on living I heard expressed in AA, which on first hearing I had thought to be outrageous, if not anarchic, began after a while to make some kind of sense; this despite them being at odds with everything I had been brought up to believe was right and proper.

I had taken my first uncertain steps as a man "born from above".

About then I saw a new light. The mothballed Sunday school teachers who told me that to be born again is to be saved had been mistaken. They could not have had the experience themselves. I saw that to be born from above is not to be saved; it is not to arrive at any kind of end, or even at a beginning; it is not to find a signposted highway to a brilliant future. If my own experience was in any way typical then being born from above is not a single happening. It is a sequence of happenings. The first was my experience of the Divine Presence. As unforgettable and important as this was, there was nothing else contained within that experience. Nor could there be. It was a sense of the Divine Presence. Just that: no more. There cannot be anything more; but certainly there can be no less, because God never will withhold any part of his love.

The knowledge that I need not drink again came afterwards. The interval was small, but a clear interval there was.

From that time on, as I began to breathe the air of the new world into which I had been born, I began also to realize that old attitudes, old ways of thinking, old beliefs, old patterns of behavior, had no place in it unless I had tested them and discovered their truth for myself.

... And discovered their truth for myself!

Although comfortably more than 30 years have passed since those first stuttering days of recovery I still find myself confronted from time to time with dubious attitudes from an even earlier date. This leads me to an obvious conclusion: being born from above is less a single event than it is a first step along a joyful and never ending journey of spiritual enrichment. We are, quite literally, given the opportunity to start life all over again; to learn and to grow in the Spirit; and to experience the peace which transcends all understanding (Phil 4.7). It is to experience the peace of God, yes; it is not an exemption from suffering.

(4)

If I am correct in believing that the knowledge and experience I acquired before I was given the opportunity to start on a new life shaped the personality and character of the man I became there must have been an awful lot wrong in what I learned.

Given this it was almost inevitable that sooner or later I would point an accusing finger at my parents. They had been responsible for my upbringing; therefore they were responsible for a very large part of what I learned. While I accepted that my genetic make-up might well have inclined me towards becoming a certain kind of man I believed, as I believe now, that by far the most significant sculptor of my personality and character was the combination of influences to which I had been exposed, most especially in my infancy.

The Jesuits were well aware of the power of early influences when they coined the maxim, "Give us the boy until he is seven and we will give you the man."

Wordsworth expressed the same truth rather more elegantly when he wrote, "the Child is Father of the Man."

As I have now touched on truths well recognized by modern psychology there is perhaps little point in walking much further on such trampled ground. I will dally on one point only: understanding.

A significant part of the power of early influences is the fearsome tenacity with which they cling to their office. Even when they are identified the job of dealing with them is by no means done. Has a particular influence been benign or malign? If benign, can it be developed? If malign, can it be neutralized or reversed? If so, how? More on this anon. For the moment it may be useful if we look at just a handful of the more energetic influences that propelled me in the direction of a chaotic adult life. These were of two kinds. There were those of the sort we have discussed already, which might be regarded as calculated. Parents, grandparents, aunts, uncles, teachers: they all brought their own influences to bear on me, as they do on all of us.

There are then the influences we may choose to call accidental. As the products of situations arising in daily life these are infinite in their variety and cannot be predicted. They may be laid on us for no more than an instant, or they might form a part of our lives for days, weeks, months, or even years.

Many such accidental influences might better be described as traumas. Their effects can be, and sometimes are, severe and lasting.

(5)

A typical calculated influence is one which aims to teach a child the difference between right and wrong. Conscientious parents and others are diligent in this and must be applauded for their motives. But! The degree of success in any attempt to teach a child the difference between right and wrong must necessarily be proportionate to the teacher's own understanding of what is right and what is wrong. This is to say nothing of the numerous instances in which there is no clear cut right or wrong. These are many.

Few would dispute the need to teach children that it is wrong to launch a physical attack on someone, or to steal, or to lie. It is also probably a good thing for them to be informed at an appropriate point in their development of the hazards inherent in committing adultery or envying others their possessions - but!

Yet again that but!

Life is seldom so simple; there are so many shades of gray between black and white.

Perhaps only a very small part of how we behave is capable of expression in such clear cut terms. We need only to look back on our own lives to be reminded of how many temptations and difficulties lie in the path of the youngster. Developing sexual awareness is an obvious case in point. This arises quite naturally without help or hindrance from any external source. The possible external sources of temptation and difficulty are legion. Peer pressure is one of the more obvious examples. This can, and often does, compel youngsters in directions that are at variance with the standards and values commended in their homes.

Can children, most especially adolescents, be equipped to cope satisfactorily with these conflicting pressures? By satisfactorily I mean without being burdened with handicaps they will be doomed to carry into adult life. What is sure is that a dogmatic, "You must do this," or, "You must not do that," is doomed to failure, be it repeated a thousand times. I know, I have been there. It killed me and it has killed countless others. It still does. Yet still we do it. I have neither the wisdom nor the knowledge to suggest how further deaths might be avoided. All I can do is to share with you one of the great yearnings of my own formative years. It was probably the greatest.

There was nothing I wanted more than to be able to talk freely with my parents about the million and one thoughts, ideas, questions and adolescent embarrassments by which I was besieged. I should imagine that not one of them was a mite different from those of other youngsters of my age. I tried to talk - jumping Jehoshaphat! how I tried - but my every effort was turned back. "Don't be silly" was a typical response; "Just don't think about it" another; "No you can't" and "You must" still others. All, without exception, were unhelpful. I can see now that the effect of each turning back was twofold. It packed yet more explosive into the psychological and emotional time bomb created by its predecessors. It also blocked further the channel of self-giving until, ultimately, it was impossible for me to give anything of my deeper self to anyone. Once that had happened the timer on the bomb was triggered, for when self-giving is impossible death cannot be far distant. This was true for me. I believe it to be true for everyone.

(6)

I should like now to illustrate the above points by quoting directly from the only life whose intimacies are available to me: my own. (Please do not confuse this with an unhealthy self-obsession.)

This creates a very special difficulty. In the last 12 and more years of their lives I loved my parents dearly. I was glad I was able to be of some use to them and glad I was able to be with them both when they died. I had not always known this love. For many years our relationship was punctuated by long periods during which I came very close to hating them. At times I think I did.

Be that as it may, it is the love I had for my parents in their latter years which poses my present problem. I find myself recoiling from the idea of criticizing them by criticizing my upbringing, yet criticize I must.

I believe they made some very serious mistakes. If I fail to outline what I believe to be the most relevant of these and what I see as their consequences I cannot show the miracle of 23 April 1977 in its proper light. This I must do, for let there be no doubt on this count: I believe more strongly than I believe anything else that that light was the same Light as the one which illuminated the life of Jesus Christ throughout his earthly ministry.

With this in mind, I do not intend, here or elsewhere, to go into any more detail of what I perceive to have been my parents' mistakes than I believe to be absolutely necessary. What is more, I do recognize at all times that what I understand to be a fault of my parents may, in fact, be a deficiency in my understanding. It is also very important that I acknowledge without reservation that my parents always acted in what they sincerely believed to be my best interests.

(7)

I have already touched on one of my very earliest memories: that of my mother's oft repeated demand that I should be a good boy and a credit to her and my father. Her insistence was such that it is possible without exaggeration to substitute "saint" for "good boy". She continued to insist on my conformity with her impossible standards until the time I left home. Even then I was not immune from her suggestions.

There was just one thing in which I conformed almost willingly with my mother's standards: the effort I put into my schoolwork. At home I devoted many hours to it: in the fifth and sixth forms at grammar school I worked for 5 hours an evening, 6 evenings of the week; and for 4 hours on Saturday and Sunday mornings. Only rarely was this routine broken. Outside of schoolwork my repeated failures to achieve my mother's required standards of behavior resulted in me living with a more or less permanent sense of guilt. This was so well developed that there came a time when I suffered for thoughts I never expressed in either word or deed. The "bad" thought was in itself sufficient to distress my conscience.

*

The time has come to give a little thought to love; in particular, to love within the family. I grew up understanding it to be something expressible only in terms of duty done. It had no connection with the heart. Open displays of affection were just not on, which was why I never saw my parents kiss. How sad.

My mother loved my father because she cooked for him, washed and ironed his clothes, and kept the house immaculately clean. My father loved my mother because he brought in the money that enabled her to buy the food she cooked, the soap flakes and the starch. They loved me because they fed and clothed me, gave me a bed to sleep in and directed every single aspect of my life. My one responsibility was to show my love for them with gratitude and obedience. If I expressed my gratitude for all they did for me with unquestioning obedience, I loved them. If I did not then love them I did not. As I was frequently told that I was both ungrateful and selfish it followed that I did not love them.

More guilt.

*

Guilt! It hung like a dense black cloud over everything I thought and did. My parents used it as a weapon of control. How well I remember comments such as, "You can't love us or you would do this (or that)." There was a variation: "We won't love you if you don't do this (or that)."

Emotional blackmail though it undoubtedly was, it worked.

One result of all this was that as I became sexually aware I did not dare to talk to anyone about what was happening in and to my body. Silence did nothing to relieve my guilt, for one person and one person only was responsible for the depravity into which I had sunk - me.

The fantasies I had about girls were many: what they looked like under their clothes; what it was like to kiss one; to touch one; to - to what? What was it that, somewhere down the line, you did to or with girls? I didn't know; I honestly didn't; but my imagination, my thoughts! They caught fire and propelled me along the way to a certain hell. More guilt.

(8)

I should now share with you something of two accidental influences that played a crucial role in shaping my sickness. Both now play a significant part in my increasing health. The difference is one of awareness. As a sick man getting sicker I was not aware of the power of these influences (or traumas). Now I am. The opening of my eyes came as a gift of God, a fruit of the moment when I was born anew, from above, and given the opportunity to grow, with Jesus leading the way.

We need to go back to the time I entered the sixth form of the grammar school I attended for seven years. It seemed I had the world at my feet. No one doubted my ability to pass with ease the examinations necessary to secure a place at medical school. It was a formality, simply a case of going through the motions. Or so everyone thought.

What no one realized was how little confidence I had in my own abilities. No one could possibly have guessed how much I envied my classmates their lives. They had girlfriends; they went dancing; they talked easily with one another; knew jokes by the dozen and how to tell them; and their pocket money dwarfed mine. They did as a matter of course things about which I could only dream.

I seethed with envy, discontent and rebellion, but it was rare indeed for me to allow even as much as a hint of my true feelings to surface. Never did I allow it to be known how many doubts I harbored about the prospect of pursuing a career in medicine.

Looking back it is quite incredible that I could ever have been as passive and as malleable as I was throughout most of my adolescence. I thought rebellion, yes, and I felt rebellious; but I was a rebel who dared not openly to take up arms, for to obey my elders without question was the sum and substance of my conditioning. It was the way in which my parents had themselves been raised.

A lot of time was to pass before I even began to appreciate the profound implications of that one fact. When I eventually did the wisdom was not mine.

So, when I entered the sixth form the appearance of having the world at my feet was deceptive. In truth, a storm was brewing but, at the start of that first semester, the skies were a clear blue, the sun warm, the air fresh.

The first cloud appeared low on the horizon a day or two before we broke up for the Christmas holidays. It had the rather surprising shape of mock entry examinations. This rehearsal for the first round of the real thing (the examinations would be taken over two years) would be staged immediately upon our return to school after the seasonal break, our form master told us.

There was no reason at all for me to fear these tests or to make any special preparations for them. I was well on top of my work. Nonetheless, I was preparing for them and had been for a week or two, very thoroughly and very much to a timetable; which was why our form master's announcement threw me completely off balance. It changed an earlier arrangement which had scheduled these mocks for a week at the end of January. My carefully planned program of revision collapsed in the instant.

Mindless of the fact that I had no need to revise as I was revising and that revision time lost to me was lost equally to my classmates, I reacted furiously to the news. To everyone's amazement I jumped to my feet and protested loudly and at length about the change.

Our form master was unmoved.

"If that is the case," I shouted, when it became obvious that my objections were falling on deaf ears, "don't expect me to be here."

It was an idiotic and reckless thing to say, made memorable because normally I was as quiet as a mouse in class. My lack of confidence in the value of anything I felt inclined to say insured my silence. I mean, someone might have disagreed with me! What would I have done then?

(9)

When, too soon, the first day of the mocks arrived I woke up feeling awful. My head throbbed and every bone in my body ached. Suspecting that I had a slight temperature my mother sent me back to bed; my father was at work, so he could give no opinion. I stayed at home for the remainder of the week.

Today, rather more than 54 years after the event, it is still impossible for me to say whether or not I was genuinely sick. I do know that my fear of doing badly was so great that my mind might well have intervened and manufactured a convenient illness. Frankly, I believe it did. My classmates entertained no doubt. They remembered my threat and came to a not unreasonable conclusion. For the remaining ten weeks of the semester I was ignored by them all, apart from being abused in a variety of subtle and not-so-subtle ways. There is no need for me to elaborate on these.

I complained to no one. That would have been to go against the ridiculous schoolboy code of not telling tales.

To allow myself to be guided by the schoolboy code in such circumstances was unwise if, possibly, understandable... at school. That I failed to confide in my parents is less understandable, if more revealing. I believed then, as I still believe, that had I said anything to them I should simply have been told not to dwell on what was happening; to dismiss it from my mind and get on with my work. Such had been the prescription for every one of the very few problems I had ever tried to talk about at home. I realized many years later that the thinking behind this advice was less than profound; like, if I ignored whatever was troubling me, didn't talk about it and didn't even think about it, it would go away.

It didn't.

The inevitable happened.

Shortly before the end of the semester I collapsed.

My temperature soared to 104°F (40°C). There were no other symptoms. I lapsed into delirium and, in that condition, said enough for my parents to be able to work out the cause of my sudden illness. My mother promptly reported what I had said to the headmaster. When I returned to school at the start of the next semester everything was returned to normal; on the surface at least.

In fact normality, or normality as I knew it, was gone. Nothing would ever be the same again; for whatever may be the truth of the man I am now this man is most assuredly not a simple projection through time of the youth I was in the sixth form at grammar school. Thank God.

*

Those weeks of isolation effected many and varied changes in me. Most were superficial; some reached to the very center of my being. While I may have been vaguely aware of a small part of the superficial changes at the time those which remained hidden from my sight were, as you might expect, the ones that did the real damage. They only started on the often painful, often lengthy, but always healing process of coming into the open when alcohol became a thing of the past. Even now I should be reckless indeed to claim that all of them have emerged.

As a direct consequence of being given the opportunity to start my life afresh I gained the will and the means to root out the deeper of these changes; to see them for what they were; to accept the damage they had done and expose it to the Light which is Jesus Christ without in the process becoming morbidly self-absorbed. It has been my consistent experience that the exposure, understanding and full acceptance of whatever is responsible for the original sickness opens the way to healing. Without this exposure, understanding and acceptance healing is unlikely, if not impossible.

*

The return to an appearance of normality at the start of the summer semester did not take away my daily dread of going to school. It did not give me back the level of concentration to which I was accustomed or the interest I had lost in my studies. My academic standing slid ever downwards as my marks began to suffer. There were those among my classmates who were by no means displeased to witness this but, for the first time in my life, I didn't give a damn.

What I wanted above all else was to be accepted as one of themselves by the dominant clique among my classmates. I tried telling jokes, for the joker was held in high regard; I tried being insolent to teachers; turning in homework late and sloppily done; inventing erotic adventures with girls and playing elaborate practical jokes: anything that might achieve my desired end.

I failed miserably because nothing I did was natural to me. Just about all of my efforts brought me into conflict with the whisperings of my true self, to which I was completely deaf.

This, then, was the first of the two traumas that changed the course of my life. The second was its child.

(10)

At about the time the pain of isolation reached its peak I fell in love with a married woman I will refer to as Kate. I had been introduced to her by her son, who I knew slightly. He was in the first form at school. In the impossible hope that she might reciprocate my feelings I told Kate of my love. To my astonishment she neither ridiculed nor rejected me. On the contrary, she could not have been more understanding. Before long I began to see her understanding as encouragement. Still she did not ridicule or reject me.

From then on nature took its course regardless of the age difference between us, regardless of social differences, regardless of anything bearing any resemblance to sanity.

It mattered not to me that she was almost exactly twice my age, or that she had two children, or that she was separated from her RAF officer husband and divorce proceedings were in hand. All I cared about was that I was loved by a beautiful, educated, cultured woman of the world who spoke with the voice of an angel. It is little wonder that I idolized Kate, for she listened to everything I had to say and made me believe that what I said had value. No one had ever done that. Better still, perhaps best of all, she introduced me with great good humor and no little tact to a new and exciting world of ideas; to a way of thinking that was to my inhibited mind nothing short of revolutionary. She also coached me in some of the more basic social graces. In these I was utterly lacking.

And all she did she did with love.

Strangely, despite guilt having been such a burden over the years I have never felt guilty about my relationship with Kate, nor do I regret it. It taught me a lesson beyond price: the transforming power of unconditional love. I should like you to be quite clear about this: it was not her subsequently questionable love for me that had the power to transform, but my unconditional love for her.

At this moment I am very conscious of a passage from the well known prayer credited to St. Francis:

"Divine Master, grant that I may not so much seek
to be consoled, as to console;
to be understood, as to understand;
to be loved, as to love."

Think carefully. Please. Could it be that St. Francis is suggesting that it is the going out from self in love that has the power to transform: the lover, certainly; the beloved, possibly? I believe so. It is the truth of my own experience.

Kate also introduced me to qualities of thought and behavior, and to the beauties (or truths) of literature and music, which I might otherwise never have discovered. Can it be coincidence that my very earliest outward interests in recovery from alcoholism revolved around literature and music?

Kate lifted me from a world in which nothing had value unless it could be priced to one in which that with the greatest value could not be priced and always came as a gift. I did not know it at the time, nor could I, nor, I should imagine, did Kate, that this world is the world of Jesus. It is the world he urges us to seek, for in that world our treasures cannot be destroyed by moth and rust, nor can thieves break in and steal them. Is it, then, surprising that the most prominent by far of the few values and standards of my earlier life I have not rejected are those to which Kate introduced me?

My parents, as you would expect, had no idea that I saw Kate at her home for an hour and so on no less than four evenings in most weeks. They thought I had taken to indulging myself in brisk, head clearing walks after finishing my studies at 10 o'clock or thereabouts. More importantly they were not aware of me starting to play truant on games afternoons in order to spend a couple of precious hours alone with Kate at her home. It was in the course of these hours that we took our first tentative steps from a joint exploration of the humanities towards an ultimately explosive sexual intimacy.

Our clandestine relationship progressed reasonably smoothly until shortly before I was due to leave school and embark on my medical studies. Then, as was almost bound to happen, rumors began to circulate. Confirmation was not long in following.

The noise of the ensuing scandal - remember, this was 1953;

sex was not discussed in polite circles - resulted in yet another decision being taken out of my hands. My entry to medical school was postponed until after I completed my two years national service in the army. Opposition was useless; the headmaster and my parents were united.

National service was, I suppose, the next best thing to the European tour of Victorian times. I cannot say truthfully that I felt any sense of shame or humiliation at having been discovered in an illicit relationship with an older and (although unknown to me) now divorced woman. Nor did I care that my entry to medical school was to be delayed by two years. I didn't care about anything or anyone but Kate. Nothing changed my love for her, which I firmly believed she reciprocated. True, she did admit to feeling shame when our relationship became generally known, but I was confident she would get over this.

For the first 6 weeks of my Army service we exchanged long loving letters. Towards the end of this time I was able to write and tell her I had been given a 48 hour pass and would be home late on the Friday evening, just four days away. She replied by return with the news that she would be out of Nottingham on urgent family business which could not be put off. I was devastated.

At home, with nothing better to do on the Saturday morning, I decided to take a walk. Chance took me by a local church where, on the lawn separating it from the road, I saw Kate standing with a man I didn't know. She wore a pale blue dress and carried a bouquet.

They were newly-weds posing for photographs.

At first I could not believe my eyes but, gradually, numbness replaced disbelief. This numbness gave way to pain only reluctantly. The whole process took months. Then it promptly went into reverse. When the cycle eventually ended I was possessed by an aching, howling, void. This became my normal condition.

(11)

While it is very tempting at this point to attempt an analysis of how and why I came to be as I was, I will not. I am no more a psychologist than I am a theologian or teacher. What is not open to question is how ill-equipped I was to meet the demands of adult life when I left home to serve my two years in the army.

I felt alienated from the world in which I was compelled to function; a man apart. Nothing I saw happening about me was any concern of mine. It lacked reality. I was no more than a spectator, without voice, vote or influence of any kind.

Never, ever, did I take the initiative in anything.

My one wish was that I should be left alone to live a quiet, trouble-free life. This would not include marriage. I was quite sure that no woman would ever want to marry me.

Let me hasten to add here that self-pity had no place in my thinking, which deficiency I more than made good as my drinking career progressed. As far as I was concerned I just did not have "it". That was a simple fact. End of story. Why cry about it?

This, then, was my condition when I began my delayed studies at medical school. I was like the proverbial fish out of water. My studies were never completed. I'll spare you the gruesome details of their ending; they can add nothing of value to what I have already shared with you.

Chapter 2

There are various reasons why I need now to look again at the part played by the "Kate factor" in the early days of my recovery from alcoholism. Among the foremost of my memories of those days is the eagerness with which I looked forward to being able to read books of substance and to attend concerts and the theater with a heart and mind free of alcohol. I also fantasized for hours on end about living the life of the cultured, civilized and well-to-do bachelor. The fact that I was unemployed, broke and aiming to be reconciled with my wife, from whom I was still separated, disturbed me not at all. The financial cost of the sort of life I had in mind and the difficulties I was encountering in finding work likewise failed to undermine my equilibrium.

These, though, were the very early days of my recovery; a time when most of my thoughts and ambitions were born in the land of the fairies, where the clouds are pink and castles are built in the air. It was a silly time in many ways but, although I did not and could not then appreciate it, my fantasy about living the life of a cultured, civilized and well-to-do bachelor was in its own oddball way helpful. It led me to make a start on reading better quality books than I had concerned myself with for years: fiction, poetry, history, devotional, philosophy, popular science, biographies of the famous and the infamous; anything and everything just as long as it had substance. On top of this I did actually begin to attend concerts and the theater. This was wonderful. Better still, I found no satisfaction in any form of superficiality. I thought as deeply as I was then capable about all I read and saw and heard. In the process I learned to recognize the many areas I should need to revisit, often more than once.

The fact is, I was feeding a hunger I had lived with for the larger part of my life without even being aware of its existence. Although I was not then conscious of it I was discovering why I had spent so many hollow years - most especially the drinking years - aching, literally aching, under the weight of an intolerable burden of emptiness. I was discovering for myself - I stress, *for myself* - that I was more than a mind and a body; that I was, like you and everyone else walking the face of the earth, essentially a spiritual being.

I was discovering *for myself* that, "Man does not live on bread alone, but on every word that comes from the mouth of God" (Matt 4.4). The words which came from the mouth of God took on substance and clothed themselves in all I read; in its meaning and in the beauty of Wordsworth, of Eliot, of Macaulay and of Ruskin. They took on substance, too, and clothed themselves in the music of Bach and Brahms, of Mozart and Mahler, of Schubert and Haydn. They were spoken pianissimo and fortissimo, in point and in counterpoint. In truth, I was besieged by a benign army of ideas and melodies drawn from the ranks of all that is beautiful and fruitful, which is all that falls from the mouth of God.

It was all tremendously, incredibly, exhilaratingly exciting. And it was all - I do not doubt it for one second - down to the presence of Jesus in my life as a constant companion and source of inspiration; or, sometimes, just sometimes, as a consolation.

*

An expanded experience of living without alcohol has brought home to me most forcibly how unerring was the guidance I received in those early days of my recovery. It awakened me to that Life which gave me life at the moment of my conception: that Life which is truly eternal.

It would not have been enough for me simply to put down the bottle and to become what, in any case, no one has yet called me: a sober, respectable, upright citizen. Although I might for a time have been able to observe the letter of the laws of respectable and responsible behavior, I should have been living on bread alone. I doubt if I should have been able to live, truly to live, after that fashion for very long. Can anyone?

(2)

The reason for me sharing with you a little about the early days of my recovery may be found in one of Jesus' teachings: "When an evil spirit comes out of a man, it goes through arid places seeking rest and does not find it. Then it says, 'I will return to the house I left.' When it arrives it finds the house unoccupied, swept clean and put in order. Then it goes and takes with it seven other spirits more wicked than itself, and they go in and live there. And the final condition of that man is worse than the first" (Matt 12.43-45).

These are cautionary words, but words that reflect with great accuracy the truth of my experience. The expression, "evil spirit", is a part of the truth of that experience. Neither here nor anywhere else do I propose to use in its place any contemporary euphemism. Spades need to be called spades; and evil spirits nothing but evil spirits.

In my own case the evil spirit referred to by Jesus was made manifest in alcoholism: alcoholism, not alcohol. Alcohol was the anodyne, not the pain. Still less was it the illness. The analogy is simple. When I was relieved of the need to take alcohol in a vain effort to deaden the pain of alcoholism, my house - by which I mean the deepest part of my being; you may call it my soul if you wish - was left unoccupied. It had also been swept and tidied. Fortunately it did not for long remain in that condition. My involuntary Spirit led craving for the life of the cultured and civilized bachelor prompted me to begin almost at once on furnishing it with the insights of great literature and filling its spaces with the melodies and inspiration of the music of genius. Most importantly, the whole was brought into a healing harmony in the silence of the Quaker Meetings for Worship which I then attended, the time I dedicated to my private devotions and my then considerable involvement in AA.

When the evil spirit returned in the form of periodic cravings for alcohol I liked to imagine its frustration as being of a kind with that of the big bad wolf arriving at the brick house built by the three little pigs: he huffed and he puffed, and he huffed and he puffed, but for all he huffed and for all he puffed, the house stood; its doors stayed firmly locked and bolted. Is this story not reminiscent of what Jesus said about the wise man who built his house on rock: "The rain came down, the streams rose, and the winds blew and beat against that house; yet it did not fall, because it had its foundation on the rock" (Matt 7.25)?

Yet again experience is exactly in line with Jesus' teaching: but, as is so often the case, this only became apparent in hindsight. I'm quite sure that neither the story of the return of the evil spirit nor that of the house built on rock would have meant a thing to me at any time before 23 April 1977.

History had to precede understanding.

I am devoted to Jesus. I believe him to be the greatest spiritual guide ever to have lived. Even so, no matter how wise or explicit his words may be, and what he said about the return of the evil spirit could hardly have been more explicit, they are sterile unless and until they are related to life. And to what life can any of us better relate his words than to the one which we call our own?

Almost without exception this means that we learn at the very deepest level, the life changing level, only by making mistakes. At a first reading this may seem to be negative or depressing. In fact it is a statement that reflects something tremendously positive and exciting.

It is a very short step from here to seeing ignorance as the root of a great many of the evils and misfortunes that befall us even if the ignorance is not our own. Take a look, if you will, at the example to be found at 1 Timothy 6.9-10: "People who want to get rich fall into temptation and a trap and into many foolish and harmful desires that plunge men into ruin and destruction. For the love of money is a root of all kinds of evil." Could it be that the love of money is preceded by ignorance of a more constructive ordering of priorities?

Let me take this thinking one step further and suggest a short sequence of truths: error is the product of ignorance, but without ignorance there is nothing to be learned; and without learning there can be no spiritual growth. Another less obvious truth may be added to this chain: without spiritual growth we cannot achieve our full potential as human beings. This is most certainly not the same as achieving all of which we are capable in our careers - but the two do not need to be mutually exclusive.

These considerations help me to understand better what Jesus might have had in mind when he said, "It is not the healthy who need a doctor, but the sick" (Luke 5.31).

It is very dangerous, I believe, for anyone - and I do mean anyone - to think of themselves as a complete person, perfectly balanced, self-sufficient and in need of help from no one. And never, never, I beg you, fall into the trap of trying to project an image of yourself that pretends to such self-sufficiency. There is absolutely nothing anywhere in this book that I can suggest to you as a subject more deserving of your earnest and urgent consideration than this.

Let me return your attention once more to the Prologue and the moment I said to my mother, "I need help." I received the help I so badly needed because those three words were far, far, more than an intellectual admission that something had me beaten and that I didn't have a clue what to do or where to go. It was an admission and an acceptance that welled up with volcanic force from the very depths of my being. It was an eruption, a shout, a scream, a pleading, that was, and will probably remain, the greatest and most important truth I have ever spoken about myself. It tore me wide open, but, in the tearing it opened me to the healing love and presence of none other than God.

I still need help. My whole life bears testimony to that great truth. I cannot live in total isolation, nor do I wish to, for is life not all about relationships? May it not even be defined in terms of relationships: the relationships we have within ourselves; with God (for me, with God through Jesus); and then the relationships we have with our families, friends, acquaintances and the material world, the environment in which we live?

The order in which I list these relationships is rather one of convenience than importance, for there can be no relationship more important than the one we have - or don't have! - with God. For me the state of this most important of relationships varies according to whatever is the current state of the network of internal relationships existing between my mind, emotions, spiritual life and body. The more these are in harmony the more in harmony is my relationship with God likely to be, and the more likely I am to enjoy good relationships with the people I meet and with the world in which I live. Such has been my experience.

Let me dwell for a while on the network of different relation-ships existent within ourselves. Correction. Let me dwell for a while on the network of different relationships within myself; not because I am the most fascinating person I know, the only one in whom I have any interest, but because I am the only person whose history I can quote with authority. Only I can speak with first hand knowledge of how it happened that the different relationships within me finally came to be arranged in some sort of reasonable order.

This should be looked at closely, for in it I can see glittering the key to a spiritual life that is not only active and progressive, but exciting. I do mean exciting. I am convinced beyond all doubt that it can and should be the most adventurous and fulfilling undertaking upon which anyone can embark. Anyone, mark you.

The key is a master key. It fits all locks. Try it.

I will give to this key a name: Rigorous Self-honesty. I can allow pretense no place in my heart or mind. If I am angry, I need to be able to recognize and to admit to that anger. If I am full of hate, worry, fear, resentment, bitterness, depression or despair; or if I am happy, hopeful, confident and, possibly, flying on cloud nine; it matters not. Whatever my condition, I need to be able to recognize it and to admit to it; to myself if to no one else, and to do so without justification, excuse, condemnation or self-congratulation.

This is all very fine and noble, or it might be were it not for an awkwardness that tends to dull the self-righteous righteous shine of my fineness and nobility. It's called truth. I am a committed Christian, yes, but this does not alter by one jot the fact that I am human and subject to all human frailty. For this I thank God even though it means there are times when I would rather not admit to my anger, or that I am full of hate, or worry, or fear or what-have-you; which means there are times when I will try to convince myself that I am not angry, or full of hate, or worry, or fear or what-have-you. As things are I thank God that I have an awareness of these frailties because that awareness allows me also to be aware of the guidance made available to me - as it is to all of us - by the Spirit of Truth, the Holy Spirit.

"... when he, the Spirit of truth, comes, he will guide you into all truth... He will bring glory to me by taking from what is mine and making it known to you. All that belongs to the Father is mine" (John 16.13-15).

The point I am laboring to make is that for as long as I refuse to face the truth of what is happening inside me I can know no peace. The web of relationships between my mind, heart, body and soul will be out of kilter, as will be my relationship with God. I may even feel positively ill or exhausted. It has happened. It may be a part of your experience too.

It is only when I take time out to listen in prayerful silence to what is happening inside me - to listen without thought or comment, that is, and with heart and mind turned to God - that I can even begin to hope for peace to be restored.

But: "Prayerful silence."

Ouch!

It sounds so obnoxiously pious and religious, doesn't it? It could even be that it makes me sound like one of the mothballed Sunday school teachers of my younger days, or as though I'm on a spiritual high. I am neither, believe me. I am speaking of something I do every day of my life, for the good and simple reason that it is the one sure way I know of getting the most from every day.

If that still sounds obnoxiously pious and religious, so be it.

(3)

I have spoken of Rigorous Self-honesty as the key to an active and exciting spiritual life. "I can allow pretense no place in my heart or mind," I wrote. "If I am angry I need to be able to recognize and to admit to that anger... without justification, excuse, condemnation or self-congratulation." Let me now expand on that statement.

I must doubt if I should ever have been able to recognize the essential elements of the turmoil within me prior to being freed of the compulsion to drink without Divine assistance. (For Divine you may read God, Jesus or the Holy Spirit if you wish.) The same is true of most, if not all, of what I have learned since. So, when I admit to myself my fears and my anger; my wrongs, shortcomings and what-have-you, I am in fact returning to God truths He has revealed to me. I do no less when I recognize that I have got something right or done something worth doing.

By far the best example I can quote of the working out of this principle may be found in what happened on that life changing morning in April 1977. The three words I addressed to my mother, "I need help", were, at one and the same time, an admission of the truth, an unconditional acceptance of it and a prayer for deliverance. For a number of years that was the sum of my understanding.

Now I believe I see a little more clearly. Yes, "I need help" was a prayer. But it was more. For in admitting and accepting without reservation the truth of my alcoholism I was delivered from it.

Since then I have observed the working out of the same sequence of happenings time and time and time again. It seems that once I have understood and accepted a truth without condition or qualification of any kind it penetrates to the innermost reaches of my being and becomes an essential part of me. From then on I can do no other than always to respond in affirmation of that truth in every department of my life.

This is not to be held captive; it is to be granted a freedom. And what is true for me is true for you.

What I cannot afford to forget, though, is that it is God who enables me to recognize the truth in the first place. In admitting and accepting this truth I return it to God and so accede to my own deliverance.

*

All I have shared with you over the last several pages began with a few thoughts and memories circulating around Jesus' description of what happens when an evil spirit comes out of a man and wanders through arid places seeking rest. On this occasion the understanding I have of Jesus' words does not arise only in my own experience, which has been good. It also has its origins in a tragedy to which I was a close witness. Because I believe that a creative understanding of the point Jesus makes is so important and such a vital ingredient of the good life, I feel I must, this once, share with you a part of what I know of someone else's tragedy.

The someone else was a friend in AA with whom I had the closest relationship it is possible for one person to have with another without sex being involved. He was a man I will call Dublin.

Before I can usefully go any further I should tell you a little about how Alcoholics Anonymous helps the newly recovering alcoholic. The newcomer to AA is encouraged to find a sponsor, a sponsor being a member well established in recovery with whom the newcomer can share those things about which he, or she, cannot bring themselves to speak in an ordinary meeting. All alcoholics have plenty of these! When I began to look around for a sponsor, I liked what I saw in Dublin. It was obvious from listening to him speak at meetings that he was well versed in AA philosophy, had his life organized, spoke fluently in a way I could understand, and that we were compatible personalities. This was all good but, of his many attributes, none impressed me more than the six or seven years of recovery he had behind him. At that time six or seven years without alcohol was, to me, only a little short of eternity.

It took me some time to screw up the courage to ask this demigod to be my sponsor, but when I did and he agreed I was over the moon. I still have the formal letter of acceptance he wrote to me.

The help I received from Dublin in the first three and a half years or so of my recovery was priceless. I could speak to him, sometimes even cry on his shoulder, at any time of night or day. He never refused me his ear or his shoulder. Though he would sometimes be blunt to the point of crudity Dublin never showed a trace of impatience at my many lunacies: and that, believe me, was in itself a testimony to the intrinsic quality of the man.

What I did not realize was that behind Dublin's formidable array of strengths there lurked a fatal weakness: excessive ambition. In his case this included a wish to make up for what he saw as the years he had lost to drinking. I am, of course, being wise after the event. Or it could be that, even now, my diagnosis of his weakness is mistaken. But there was a fatal weakness. Of that there can be no doubt.

When I was rather more than three years into recovery and starting to show the first significant signs of joining the human race Dublin left his wife. He promptly set up home with a woman with whom he said he had been conducting an affair for several months. I was shocked, both because I had believed his marriage to be as sound as a bell and because his adultery flew in the face of everything AA advises. That is to say nothing of the simple, open, lifestyle he prescribed for me.

Hard on the heels of him setting up home with Rebecca, the new woman in his life, Dublin left the firm with whom he held a senior position to set up in business as a computer systems consultant. Rebecca was to be his business as well as his sexual partner. Her father provided their capital.

Almost immediately Dublin's plans began to fall apart. Expected business did not materialize. No business materialized. Then, with a suddenness I could hardly comprehend and still find difficult to credit, my relationship with him went into reverse. He started to seek my ear at ever shorter intervals. What he told me worried me sick; yet such is the code of confidentiality within AA there was no one in whom I could confide. I believe now that I made a mistake not to share my fears with someone a lot further into recovery than me. But now is too late.

Dublin and Rebecca ran out of cash; her father would lend them no more. They were in arrears with their mortgage; their building society was pressing them hard; their bank account was well into the red; and their collection of unpaid bills beggared belief.

As bad as they were Dublin's financial problems counted for nothing when compared with his increasingly rapid loss of contact with reality. So fast was his decline that I went through a very bad few days wondering if I had got everything wrong and the one living the nightmare was not him but me.

To quote one example to illustrate the state of Dublin's mind: he complained to me that his bank was being utterly unreasonable in refusing to extend his overdraft limit. That would probably have been a valid complaint if his prediction of sales worth £3,000,000 in the next three months had had any foundation in fact. The bleak truth was that he had generated not a single pound's worth of business in the previous three months. No sane person would have forecast anything different for the next three.

Dublin began to regret leaving his wife, but at no time did he accept any responsibility for his decision. It was all Rebecca's fault; she had seduced him. From there he reasoned that a woman who would deliberately break up a marriage was capable, or incapable - whichever suited his purpose - of anything. And so he heaped on Rebecca's shoulders all responsibility for the parlous state of their business.

There are no words to describe my dismay as Dublin's flight from reality progressed. It soon became impossible for me to maintain any sort of rational contact with him.

I learned later that his two sons from his first marriage (the wife he left to be with Rebecca was his second) had been taken into care; that Rebecca had left him; that his home had been repossessed; and that he was living in a rooming house with a female alcoholic. They were both said to be drinking heavily.

There followed a period of a few months during which I heard no more of Dublin. He had disappeared. Then one day the telephone rang and the AA member on the other end of the line told me he was dead. He had hanged himself.

(4)

Excessive ambition was a fatal flaw lurking behind the supercompetent image which Dublin projected when I first knew him. There were others, but it is only in very recent years that I have perhaps come anywhere near to understanding fully the part they played in his ultimate downfall. I hope most sincerely that I am not doing an injustice to Dublin's memory to share with you my thoughts about these flaws. I do so because I believe an understanding of what they involve is essential to spiritual growth. As always I will be speaking of the truth of my experience.

I recognized early in my relationship with Dublin - he made no secret of it - that he was ambitious. I saw neither harm nor danger in this, or not in his case. To me he was a fully rounded and well balanced man. I saw not one chink in the armor in which he clothed himself.

As time passed it occurred to me that I had never heard Dublin admit to being wrong in anything. For a while this troubled me, but not for long. I persuaded myself that, as he was my sponsor, it might not be a good thing for him to admit error; or not to me.

I had a lot to learn.

The quality of what Dublin shared with me was, in retrospect, also very much open to question. It was not until I came to weigh the pros and cons relating to the inclusion of his story in this narrative that I realized what it was in his sharing that so often failed to carry conviction after I stopped looking on him as a demigod. He knew the AA program of recovery inside out; he could quote from AA literature by the yard and expand at length on the thinking behind every facet of AA philosophy. What I very seldom heard him do was to share his own thoughts, feelings and experiences. Very little came from his heart; there was virtually no spontaneity in any of his sharing. He remained imprisoned within the walls of intellectualization, an establishment from which it is very difficult to escape. Ego is its governor.

True, his house had been swept clean. For several years he had not taken any alcohol: but abstinence alone was not sufficient to save him. I must doubt if anything which excludes the Spirit ever can be, either for the recovering alcoholic or for anyone else. If we wish to live fully as free men and women, to feel that Life which is the source of life pounding through our veins, we surely need to feed on more than bread. For whatever reason Dublin never grasped this. He tried to live on bread alone which, in his case, was a considerable intellect.

To the best of my knowledge he never shared his doubts, fears, mistakes, the extent of his faith (or lack of it), or whatever he thought of as his strengths and weaknesses, with anyone. Based on the evidence of the latter months of his life it is doubtful if he admitted them even to himself. Had he only done this, even in part, and then taken the next step - to admit to another human being that which he admitted to himself - there were so many who would have gladly lent him an understanding ear, for as long and as often as he needed it.

*

We cannot live to ourselves alone. Of that I am quite certain. Whether or not we recognize it I believe we all have a need of at least one other person in whom we can confide any part of what we think and feel; however black it may seem to be, or actually be: our fears, our failings, our hopes and our strengths. We need also to be receptive and sensitive to what others may wish to confide in us. If life is about nothing else - and I believe it is about a lot else - it is about relationships. It is a part of my experience that the quality of any life and any relationship is always the greater and the more joyful if there is present in it that which transcends bread alone: God.

If that which transcends bread is absent from our lives then although not all will share Dublin's fate - very few do, thank God

- we shall give muscle to Henry Thoreau's familiar maxim, "The mass of men lead lives of quiet desperation."

This is not the life Jesus would have any of us live. It is not the life any of us need to live.

(5)

A postscript.

The subjective account I have given of Dublin's last months and my relationship with him is only a fraction of the story as I know it. In deciding which parts to include and which to leave out, and in the writing itself, I set in train all sorts of memories and emotions. I also brought into the light attitudes I had until then chosen to hide away as best I could. Once exposed I knew I should not ignore them. And so I didn't. I couldn't. They would not go away. What is more, I was bound to recognize the element of discord that my reaction to their unconscious influence had introduced into my otherwise harmonious marriage. Let me share with you what is on my mind.

For many years I professed a lack of concern about the size of my income; that I could think of no way of life more tedious than one dedicated to the pursuit of cash. I was able to point to a track record reaching back for more than 25 years which, outwardly at least, gave ample evidence in support of the sincerity of my profession.

Unfortunately the track record is silent about the times when a craven desire for material wealth bubbled disagreeably to the surface of my consciousness. It ignores the fact that on the occasions this happened my whole personality changed. The man I became really was a most unpleasant character, envious of those living in more privileged circumstances than himself and resentfully covetous of their possessions and lifestyles. He was an angry man, bitter and brimming over with self-pity; deaf to everything but the left, left, left, right, left of sour "if onlys" tramping in hobnailed boots across his mind. It was the sound of the Devil's own army on the march.

The "if onlys" refer, of course, to the brilliant and materially rewarding career in medicine this man never had, the acclaim he never won. Please, spare no tears for him. He thrives on them.

Pray God I may never forget that this man was, and is, the dark side of me.

So, I should like to be better off. But why did it take so long for the truth to surface? Now that it has, what is my genuine attitude to material wealth and the so called good things of life? And what relevance does all of this have to my relationship with God as He makes Himself known to me through Jesus? Do these questions and their answers matter to anyone other than me? I believe they do, which is why I propose to share them with you and to devote an entire chapter to the sharing.

Chapter 3

Of the questions I posed at the end of the last chapter I feel I should deal first with my present attitude to material wealth and the so-called good things of life. Attitude is perhaps not the right word. Relationship is better. The distinction I make here is that I normally think of attitude as a one way thing, a relationship as two way. Let's face it, whether we like it or not we are all involved in a relationship with materialism and the consumer society. As this relationship is one we cannot sever we need to get it right. If we do not we are storing up all manner of problems for ourselves, not the least being that we dam our spiritual development. Believe me, please; I speak from hard experience.

My own relationship with materialism is a changed one. It may be stated simply and briefly. I should like to be in a position to spend less time than I do in balancing the domestic budget. I should like, with my wife, to be able to afford a home of our own rather than the rented sheltered accommodation in which we live at the moment. I should like us to be able to install in this home one or two physical comforts for our mutual enjoyment; even a little of what is attractive to the eye. It would also be very pleasant to share the love we have with a little dog, or maybe two.

I hope these are all reasonable ambitions. As much as I should like to achieve them I am not, under any circumstances, prepared to make them the be-all and end-all of my life: ambitions that I'm prepared to do a Dr. Faustus in order to achieve. That would be plain daft. I have not forgotten Dublin.

Why has it taken me so long to admit to these very modest wishes? How is this "coming out" relevant to my relationship with God? And why on earth should I think that these largely mundane considerations might be of any interest at all to you? These are questions which cannot be answered either so briefly or so simply. They do, however, contain features that may have a bearing on your life. Unless, of course, you have already achieved a state of perfect self-honesty.

What I will be trying to do is to share with you how a measure of honest self-awareness is necessary before it is possible to turn outwards to God or to discover His kingdom within. The measure need not be large - it may indeed be tiny - nor should it be confused with an unhealthy obsession with self.

(2)

I propose to start on this stage of our joint exploration by reminding you of the two great commandments (Matt 22.37-39): "Love the Lord your God with all your heart and with all your soul and with all your mind... love your neighbour as yourself."

These, particularly the latter, are quoted so often they have been almost relegated to the status of clichés. And clichés are clichés because they are trotted out so often that few bother to take pause and to give to them any more than a passing thought.

The subject of both commandments is love. Now that is an awkward one. We normally associate love with all sorts of pleasant thoughts and feelings, not with commands. Love arises spontaneously - doesn't it? Everyone knows that. It is certainly not something we can turn on to order; nor is it a natural companion of command. Fish and chips, yes; tripe and onions, yes; bangers and mash, yes; love and command, no.

I must confess right here and now that, for many years, I stubbed my toes with painful regularity against the stumbling block of loving to command. I just didn't see how it was possible to switch on love as though it were an electric light.

And so the two great commandments crumbled into pious nonsense.

The difficulty I had in understanding what Jesus meant when he spoke of love was with the emotion and sentimentality which, in my ignorance, I attached to the word. I could hardly hear it without hearing also the lush strings of Mantovani's orchestra playing *One Enchanted Evening*. It was an ignorance that might well have had a very long future had it not been for what happened on that glorious morning of 23 April 1977.

Again that date!

Why the constant repetition?

Because it was then I experienced the perfect love of God; the perfect love that is God.

It is also true to say that on that morning I was not most people's idea of a lovable man. Heck, in the moments before I experienced the Divine Presence I was prepared to do my elderly parents a violence in order to get the money to buy the alcohol I craved. Aside from this I can think of no part of my being that was not grossly underdeveloped or warped. I lived in a world of horrendous fantasy; I was a compulsive and pathological liar; and; and; and... it was a hell of a state to be in, believe me - and hell is exactly the right word.

Despite all this God took me exactly as I was and bathed me in His love without condition or qualification. It was a love that turned my life right round and gave to it a meaning, a direction and a fullness I had never before known.

Although I do not expect ever to become as Jesus - the wrongs I continue to do and the mistakes I persist in making are legion - the meaning, direction and fullness about which I speak are, nonetheless, distilled in one sincere desire: to follow in his footsteps as best I can.

At the most critical moment of my life God filled me with His love. True. But, to repeat myself, that was all He did. There was no need for Him to do more; no need for a voice to boom down from heaven on high to tell me I had been saved and must change my ways; no demand that I should love Him in return for His love; no threat to cast me into the everlasting fires of hell if I let Him down; no task I must perform out of gratitude for what

He had done for me. No. Though I knew God's love as the most real experience I had ever had or was likely to have, it was a love freely given, demanding of nothing.

Perhaps surprisingly, perhaps not, even now, more than 30 years on, for me to recall my experience of God's love on that one morning is almost for me to re-live it. It is quite usual, as at this very moment, for me to feel the prick of tears in my eyes; occasionally to have them run down my cheeks.

This then was my greatest lesson in love. It contained all I needed to know. Its key feature - it towered (and towers) above all else - was without doubt God's acceptance of me. *He took me exactly as I was*, mountain range of warts and all, and embraced me in His love.

This is surely the love I should have for Him. I should be able to accept Him as *He* is, even though I have nothing in my mind, heart or imagination I might regard as an image of God. My mind, heart and imagination are too limited, too finite, even to make a start on shaping one. An ant gifted with the power of speech could probably make a better job of describing the geography of the earth. This troubles me not at all. I am quite satisfied to have God remain a mystery. I know all I need to know about Him to convince me of His reality: I know of His love, for I have experienced it. There is no greater gift.

I believe it is a mistake, albeit an understandable one, and surely a waste of time, to create an image of God or to attempt to define Him. Any attempt to do so is for the creature to attempt to create its creator; it is to attempt to reduce the infinite to the finite; to contain it. It is just not on. And yet many try and many invest their faith in a God of their own creation. But is a faith in a created God a faith that will stand the test of life? Can a created God stand unchanged and constant through whatever trials may come? Will a created God stand unchanged and constant as we make our mistakes and commit our wrongs?

We might do well to remember here the words of the prophet

Isaiah (29.16): "You turn things upside down, as if the potter were thought to be like the clay! Shall what is formed say to him who formed it, 'He did not make me'? Can the pot say of the potter, 'He knows nothing'?"

(3)

Do you understand yet what relevance these few reflections on the need to accept God as He is have to the difficulties I had in facing the truth of my relationship with material wealth? Can you yet see, in your own experience, how ridiculous it is to create any image of God? Can you see how my mistakes might have a bearing on your life?

Please do not answer yes if no is the truth.

I believe my refusal to accept the truth of my attitude to material wealth was a direct consequence of my failure to appreciate the overwhelming generosity of God's love. And that despite the experience I had had of it! This same failure speaks volumes of how, despite my superficial awareness of the impossibility of constructing an adequate image of God, there lurked in my unconscious an image of Him as a stern and demanding father figure. Given this it is hardly surprising that my conscious mind so readily embraced what it mistakenly conceived to be the "proper" attitude to material wealth. What rot! Understandable rot, but rot all the same: and deluded rot to boot.

How say you?

(4)

"If you hold to my teaching, you are really my disciples. Then you will know the truth, and the truth will set you free" (John 8.31-32).

Those familiar words are especially appropriate at this point in our travels because they state a profound truth of my experience. They also direct my thoughts to the dishonesty which, I feel and fear, all too often obscures Jesus from my view. It may be the same with you.

Let me briefly try to make clear an important part of my own position. Not since I was a child have I believed Jesus to be the one and only Son of God, conceived by the Holy Spirit and born of the Virgin Mary. Nor do I believe some of the other things said about him. The lazy side of me, the conformist side, wishes I could. My life would probably be a lot more comfortable were I able to embrace one of the Christian creeds as a statement of facts, but I can't - or not yet.

This is a simple truth.

There is no point in me pretending otherwise.

No pretense holds good before God.

Any attempt at pretense separates me from God.

Amazingly - how I wish I could find a way of getting across to you how amazing I believe the truth of it to have been - this disbelief was a part of the me so miraculously bathed in the love of God on the one morning 30 odd years ago! I was neither dammed nor damned for my skepticism. I was loved. And how I was loved! Me! An alcoholic loser; a down and out; a pain in the backside, no use to man or beast: but I was loved.

(God loves you no less, dear friend, whoever and whatever you are; however much or however little you may think of yourself. Believe me! Please!)

To return to Jesus: if I cannot accept as the truth some of the things said about Jesus; if I cannot understand all he has to say for and about himself; however complicated the knots I tie myself up in when I contemplate his life on earth, I can and do see in him the very incarnation of God's love.

That *is* something.

It is quite something, for there is no greater, more liberating or more universal truth than God's love, nor can there be. It simply is. And never do we see it demonstrated more clearly than in the life, death and resurrection of Jesus Christ and in the Life that is his Word; for he is the Word and he is Life. And that Life is Love.

Now I must move on.

(5)

If acceptance is an essential ingredient of love so, too, is giving; a total, nothing-held-back, giving; a complete and trusting emptying of the self before the beloved... or into the beloved. I mean this quite literally.

At the lowest point in my life God accepted me as I then was, without condition or qualification. I have said as much before; I shall probably say it again. Let me now add something: God gave Himself to me; He emptied Himself before me; He emptied Himself in me. This is no mere battery of words or rhetoric for rhetoric's sake. Rather more than 30 years of reflection have led me to recognize in all I have thought and said about that morning a factual, if inadequate, description of an event I can only regard as nothing less than miraculous.

(6)

To summarize: when I speak of God's love for me I speak of a love that accepts me exactly as I am. That love is His all. I do not enjoy some kind of Divine privilege. As God loves me, so He loves you.

The more I come to understand and appreciate these truths of God's love, the more I am challenged; for if this is how I am loved, it is how I need to love if I would conform with the two great commandments. Money, property, favor, influence: even if I had them to give they are dispensable; they have no part to play in love.

Perhaps this takes us a little closer to the meaning of the first of the great commandments: "Love the Lord your God with all your heart and with all your soul and with all your mind" (Matt 22.37).

How easy it is to read these words as, "Love the Lord your God with everything you have and everything you are; you should give Him your very Self."

Quite an order.

I can't love like that. I find it impossible to imagine a time when I might, in this life at least. You may share my difficulty. Even so, inadequacy is no excuse for not making the effort. God only knows, there is little enough love in the world. However small the portion we add it is better than nothing. Nor should we forget that miracles do happen. Did Jesus not cause quite a stir when he made a few loaves and fishes go a lot further than anyone expected or would have believed possible? Who can say how far our little bit of love might stretch, or to what it might lead? Only God.

(7)

Let us now take a look at the second great commandment: "Love your neighbor as yourself."

I said earlier in this chapter that in experiencing God's love I became aware of how complete was His acceptance of me *as I then was and, subsequently, at every point in my progress towards the (still very imperfect) man I am now. It is also true that in offering Himself to me He offered everything He is, which is pure Love.*

I have also said that I am not capable of loving like that. But isn't love of this caliber precisely the example the crucified Jesus sets before us? Is it not the example set by his entire life? Is it not a love that makes Jesus' life unique in the history of the world?

Yes, yes - and yes.

Does the second great commandment tell me to love my neighbor as Jesus loves him? No. It tells me to love my neighbor *as myself.*

As myself! Two words well worth repeating; well worth emphasizing; well worth pondering deeply, very deeply indeed.

But what if I can't accept and live with myself as I am; exactly as I am without condition or qualification, and without comparing myself in any way with anyone else anywhere in the world?

The answer is clear: I do not love myself as I am loved by Jesus. It's as simple as that. Nor can I love my many billions of neighbors as Jesus loves them. *I can only love them as I love myself;* that is, as much, and in the same way, as I love myself; which is an estate too defective to be deserving of the name of love. Titles akin to hate and indifference spring more readily to mind.

Think on.

Join me if you will in another slow walk around the same idea.

Jesus tells me that I should love my neighbor(s) as myself. I wonder if there was a faint smile on his lips the first time he spoke these words? He knew full well that none of us can do otherwise. Is it not the case that our attitude to our neighbors is a very reliable reflection on how we feel about ourselves? It's true for me; I rather fancy it's true for you. Many are the times that Jesus tries to get across what was essentially the same message; he returns to it time and time again. It may perhaps be summarized in two parts, the one the mirror image of the other:

"As you regard others, so you regard yourself; as you are to others, so you are to yourself;" and

"As you regard yourself, so you regard others; as you are to yourself, so you are to others."

It is one more example of the Principle of Reciprocation; a kind of Newtonian third law of spirituality.

Let me quote a few more examples of what Jesus had to say on the subject:

"Do not judge, and you will not be judged. Do not condemn, and you will not be condemned. Forgive, and you will be forgiven. Give, and it will be given to you. A good measure, pressed down, shaken together and running over, will be poured into your lap. For with the measure you use, it will be measured to you" (Luke 6.37,38).

"Do to others as you would have them do to you" (Luke 6.31).

"Heal the sick, raise the dead, cleanse those who have leprosy, drive out demons. Freely you have received, freely give" (Matt 10.8).

"... when you give to the needy, do not let your left hand know what your right hand is doing, so that your giving may be in secret. Then your father, who sees what is done in secret, will reward you" (Matt 6.3,4).

"Ask and it will be given to you; seek and you will find; knock and the door will be opened to you. For everyone who asks receives; he who seeks finds; and to him who knocks, the door will be opened" (Matt 7.7,8).

"I tell you the truth, unless an ear of wheat falls to the ground and dies, it remains only a single seed. But if it dies it produces many seeds. The man who loves his life will lose it, while the man who hates his life in this world will keep it for eternal life" (Jn.12.24,25).

In each of the above examples there can be seen a part of the Principle of Reciprocation: "as you regard others, so you regard yourself; as you are to others, so you are to yourself." In Jesus' words, "... with the measure you use, it will be measured to you." But what standard can we use other than the only standard we have? And is the only standard we have not the standard we have been given? Think back, please, to Chapter 1 and our exploration of the ways in which we are all conditioned.

Please, do not hurry your thoughts; let them evolve and take on shape and substance in their own time. Allow them to wander as they will through those parts of your life you recalled as you read Chapter 1 and find in them more of that which will guide you ever closer to the truth of yourself.

To give what little assistance I can in this sometimes painful process, I propose, in the next section, to share with you how I was able to start working towards the truth of the other part of the Principle of Reciprocation: "As you regard yourself, so you regard others; as you are to yourself, so you are to others."

(8)

We have so far looked at the two great commandments in isolation. I doubt if we should leave them there, for there can surely be nothing in our spiritual lives that stands alone.

However deeply we may bury the truths of our self-esteem and of how and what we think of ourselves, they not only affect our relationships with our neighbors, but our relationship with God. As we can do no other than to love our neighbors exactly as we love ourselves, so we love God: until such time as the barriers standing between ourselves and God are broken down. Then, for the first time, we experience God's healing love. This is to be born anew, or from above.

If we accept this love we can begin in earnest on the long and often difficult climb towards a spiritual maturity that is almost but, I suspect, never quite an end in itself. Perhaps there never can be an end.

Perhaps - and here I would refer you to the previous chapter - the relationships within ourselves never can be completely in harmony. If this is so then spiritual maturity incorporates a simple acceptance of the fact.

But, to demonstrate just how devious the human mind can be; how deep in our unconscious the demons that separate us from God and ourselves can lurk, and how baleful the powers they have at their command; how formidable the barriers that Truth must overcome, I will dip yet again into my own experience.

The part of it upon which I will call was, in the happening, painful in the extreme and of little immediate value. A fair number of years were to pass before I realized anything like its full worth. To do that I needed help but, sure enough, the help came, and at a most opportune time.

To be more precise, it came in the course of writing the previous chapter.

On with the story.

In 1981 I was involved in what I thought at the time to be a wildly romantic affair with a female member of AA. I will call her Jenny. All the birds in creation seemed to be in full song wherever we went; our paths were strewn with cherry blossom; sweet music sounded in our ears; life was wonderful, each day a miracle. I hope you know the sort of thing I mean, whatever its outcome for you. Unfortunately for me - it seemed more like the end of the world at the time - after only four short, deliriously happy months one of Jenny's previous boyfriends returned to Nottingham, and she promptly returned to him.

I did not turn to God for help; I did not pray or even think of praying; nor did I seek solace in the Bible or any other devotional work. Instead, for a while, I turned from God for He was nowhere evident in the dark storm swept deserts that were my heart and mind. Across those bleak wastes there howled only the demons of betrayal, loss and a madness of pain. And yet God must have been present. I cannot imagine that my own will was enough to keep me from destroying myself or that it enabled me to stay clear of the bottle, for I had lost the will to live.

It was curious how, suddenly, everyone with whom I came into contact - Quakers, members of AA, my family, casual acquaintances - everyone, without exception, became hostile to me. Worse, I saw how mistaken I had been ever to credit any of them with even a mite of sense. They were all complete idiots, totally lacking in compassion and understanding.

I'm sure you get the picture.

Desperate to find someone more sympathetic to my condition than those who seemed inexplicably to have turned again me, I ventured blindly into pastures new. The pasture which most attracted me was an evangelical church. For a short while, a very short while, the ways of this church gave me some comfort. Not much, but some. Then, on an evening when I feared I was actually going mad, I telephoned one of the church's ministers at his home. The upshot of our conversation was that I arranged to see him the next morning in his office at the church.

I told Pastor M everything that had happened over the previous months, how it had all ended, and how I felt deserted by God. Every last drop of my pain, bitterness and sense of rejection - the latter was especially intense - came flooding out. One barrier was down, but another, larger and as yet unseen, remained standing.

Not for long.

Pastor M listened intently and without interruption. When at last I fell silent, exhausted by my efforts, he started to tell me about the many blessings God would grant me were I to give myself to Him without reservation. These blessings, these gifts that could be mine, sounded very good to my eager ears. But Pastor M did not stop at the simple promise. He wanted to know that I believed him. And so he asked me if I did, time and time and time again.

"These gifts could be yours Bob," he said. "Do you believe me?"

No answer.

A little more loudly: "Do you believe me? Do you believe these gifts could be yours Bob?"

No answer.

"Do you believe?"

Question... Silence.

Question... Silence.

Goodness only knows how long the dialogue between question and silence continued, but it was a long time. Eventually something in me snapped.

One final, insistent, "Do you believe?"

Then: "But that's too good for me!"

I screamed those half dozen words at Pastor M - and I do mean screamed. For a moment after they exploded from me an absolute silence descended over that office. The sob, more a howl, with which I ended the silence was almost as loud as the scream. I began to cry, then jumped from my seat and stumbled, still crying, into the street. Pastor M made no effort to stop or to follow me. I never saw him or the inside of his church again.

This scene obviously speaks loudly of my condition at the time. There is much to be learned from it but, sadly, if understandably, it was only as recently as in the preparation of the last chapter that I found the courage to look hard at it and to bring into the light its full meaning. Had I been able to do this sooner I should have been enabled to complete what unaided time never did; that is, to heal a motley collection of long-standing wounds.

Pastor M's grinding questioning came at the height of my distress following the breakdown of my relationship with Jenny. I know now that had he subjected me to the same Inquisition at almost any earlier period in my life he might well have drawn from me an identical reaction. I cannot remember any time when I truly believed, deep down, regardless of what I may have said or of any impression I may have given, that anything worth getting and keeping would ever be mine. It is not irrelevant that, until recently, and for as long back as I can remember, I regarded keeping as infinitely more difficult than getting.

There is an obvious and logical extension of this kind of thinking: why go to the trouble of getting what cannot be kept?

While this might be seen as a not altogether unreasonable point of view I should imagine there are few who would want to be identified with it. I certainly didn't. It is abysmally negative after all. So what did I do? I dug a hole deep in my unconscious, buried this most contentious of bones and forgot all about it. Easy.

Easy? Perhaps.

Understandable? Yes.

Wise? No way.

I can do nothing but shudder when I think of the number of occasions I have gone through the motions of making a sustained effort aimed at clearly defined and often worthwhile ends only - surprise, surprise - for the whole enterprise to be derailed by my own Machiavellian machinations at its very end.

Most people would feel pretty sick to have this happen with such monotonous regularity as it has happened to me, but not this man. A classic example of this may be found in an earlier book I wrote. It was a novel. It went through seven complete rewrites, the last at the behest of a literary agent, who took it on and almost immediately, for no very convincing reason, stopped trying to place it. I'll go no further into this or I'll miss the point I want to make; which is that there was a part of me, well hidden from sight, but a very large part nonetheless, that never expected the book to be published. If by some mishap it had been I do not doubt for one second that I would have predicted and embraced its failure.

My satisfaction lay in completing the task I had set myself, to see the final polished product and to know I had done the best I was then capable of doing. That was the only reward I expected, perhaps the only one that could not be taken from me. I hope I have made my point.

(9)

How did this expectation of failure or loss come about? Was it a product of my alcoholism or a part of the cause? Why could I not believe that anything good would ever be mine?

There I ran full tilt into the big one, the grandfather of the lot, the $64,000 question: why had I developed a problem with alcohol in the first place? Let me answer this one, my reasoning went, and surely everything else would immediately start to make sense.

Not an entirely unreasonable hope you might think. What can we make of it?

I think most of us have looked into our past at some time or other and tried to work out why we are where we are, and why we are what we are. I don't know about you but these are questions that tend to surface when I'm in a bit of a mess.

I discovered, as you no doubt have, that it is often possible to pick out a chain of cause and effect ending in the present. If I follow this chain back far enough, which isn't always a long journey, I can usually arrive at where "it" all started, whatever the "it" of the moment may be.

If I consider my alcoholism at a superficial level I might regard it as an effect of my upbringing. I can go on from there to reason that as my parents were the ones most responsible for my upbringing they were the originating cause of my troubles. Like, had I been allowed to develop more naturally I should probably have developed a more robust personality.

The situation that resulted in me being sent to Coventry by my classmates would probably not have arisen; or, if it had, I should have been better equipped to cope with it. I would no doubt have had an occasional adolescent romance with girlfriends of my own age, but nothing to match the traumas inherent in my relationship with Kate. And so on, and so on, until I exposed a neat and well polished chain of cause and effect.

If I go on from there and look a little more deeply into my alcoholism I can still detect a long chain of cause and effect, but it is no longer laid out in front of me in a straight line. It is bundled up and lying in a heap. The link that is the originating cause and the one that is the final effect are no longer visible. I can move the chain about, pick it up, shake it, but still find neither its beginning nor its end. Cause rubs against cause, effect against effect; one cause against several effects; one effect against several causes. All sorts of strange connections are to be found.

There are, then, the more subtle chains of cause and effect: the chains of thoughts, emotions and movements of the Spirit. They are bundled up and jammed willy-nilly into the darkest and deepest recesses of my heart, soul and mind. So tangled are their links that a psychological and spiritual shorting is a common happening, and in the shorting fresh links are created, which then join and increase the chaos.

Remember, though, I am still looking at my alcoholism as it once was, an utter confusion, a black hole in my soul from which no light escaped. Ever.

*

If you are feeling a little confused after reading the previous paragraph or two I have succeeded in my intent. Now this may seem an odd thing for a writer to say, but I've done it with a very special purpose in mind, which is to highlight what was and remains one of the great truths of my life. It is a truth that enabled me to take my first steps on the long walk to freedom (apologies to Nelson Mandela) begun on 23 April 1977.

It was only by the grace of God that I was able to begin on this walk; only the same grace enables me to continue in putting one foot in front of the other, if sometimes in no great style and if, sometimes, I lose my way altogether.

"The grace of God." A much used expression, but I can think of no better way of describing the gift that lifted me from the tangled chains of cause and effect and allowed the Spirit to flow freely through my person.

I could *not* have done it by myself. Without God I was without power. I still am.

These are truths I cannot repeat too often or too loudly.

How do they apply to you?

I do ask "how", not "if".

You need to eat and drink, as I do: we both need sleep; and we need to be able to think and to experience emotions, if we want properly to be able to describe ourselves as human. But if we - and I stress we - want to be fully human and to be able to exercise the full freedom of our humanity, do we not need help to shatter the chains of error in which we are enmeshed in order that we may rise clear of them?

Do we not *need* the grace of God?

In my own case it was a grace often called being born again, or being born from above.

You no doubt know as well as me that we do not always appreciate the value of the gifts we receive. Sometimes, if we use them at all, we do not use them for their proper purpose, or we neglect to maintain them. This is as true of spiritual gifts, received by the grace of God, as it is, say, of the toolkit or bicycle we may be given.

In the next chapter I propose to share with you how, after being given the opportunity to make a fresh start on my life, I very nearly returned myself to captivity. That I did not I owe to yet another very great gift, or grace, of God: the ability to forgive.

Chapter 4

It has been said that to bring a problem into the light is to solve it. The session I had with Pastor M did not end so satisfactorily. What emerged into the light was my absolute conviction that anything good was too good for me. That was it. No solution. End of story. Some portion of the problem was certainly exposed, but I promptly took out my spade and buried it again. My mistaken conviction that anything good was too good for me had become an essential part of my person, never to be questioned or examined.

Quite extraordinary.

There are any number of possible psychological explanations of this strange phenomenon. They are all equally false, all just so much psychobabble. The simple fact is that I lacked faith in the God who had for so long traveled quietly by my side.

I am reminded here of the story of Peter walking towards Jesus over the waters of the Sea of Galilee (Matt 14.25-33). There came a moment when he would have drowned had Jesus not reached out and taken him by the hand; just as I would so often have gone under had Jesus not reached out and given me the support I needed.

Let me now share with you two insights with which I was graced as a result of this kind of rescue act. They are separated by many years, but their combined effect has guided me to a greater freedom than any of the others from which I have been able to profit since the miracle that started me on my present way.

But a greater freedom is not absolute freedom.

(2)

I must first take you back to a period which ended with me

having an experience of the Divine Presence as great as the first. This, though, I cannot date more precisely than the Fall of 1980.

In Chapter 1 I outlined what I believed at a still early stage of recovery to be the causes of my alcoholism. These causes still stand, with very little amendment. This is not to say there has been no change. There has. It may be found in my attitude to those in whom the origins of my troubles appear to have their roots: my parents.

At one time I held them responsible for the warping of my personality and all the ills that had befallen me as a consequence of this. They were the ones ultimately to blame for the breakdown in my first marriage and the untold harm done to my children: I considered myself as being no more than the instrument of that harm. It was my parents' narrowness and lack of understanding which had condemned me to a life of poverty, insecurity and loneliness. And so on, and so on.

In a remarkably short time I managed to mix a potent cocktail of resentment, bitterness, anger and all things destructive: all directed against my parents. I convinced myself that the two people whose responsibility it had been to give me as favorable a start in life as possible had, instead, bound me hand and foot and hung lead weights around my neck. (I should point out that these very negative thoughts and feelings built to a climax only a month or two after the collapse of an unwise second marriage.)

Having reached this conclusion my relationship with my parents hit an all time low. The fault was entirely mine. What I was too blind to see was that in my eagerness to allocate blame for the ills an unkind fate had rained on me (O poor, poor, me!). I was slowly but surely preparing for a return to drinking.

Sure enough, the day came when I bought a bottle of vodka at the local liquor store. I took it home and sat and stared at it for a long, long, time. When I finally reached out to pick it up and take that lunatic first drink my right arm froze. I was quite incapable of movement. Goodness only knows - and I am speaking here of

Goodness with a capital G - how long I sat with my fingers glued to the neck of that bottle.

Then I collapsed in tears.

Seconds later the vodka disappeared down the kitchen sink.

Badly frightened, I had a well overdue word with Dublin (this was before his own difficulties became apparent). He was not pleased with me. But even when he had exhausted his vast repertoire of expletives in an effort to express the total of his displeasure he could do no more than tell me what I already knew: that I had to get rid of the resentments I had pinned on my parents. This was an absolute imperative. Under the immediate threat of the bottle nothing else mattered.

I knew the problem... Good.

I knew the answer... Better.

How to get from one to the other? I didn't have a clue.

There was also the business of being born anew. I must have been fooling myself. How could I have been reborn if I was so screwed up?

What I had forgotten was that I had never believed being reborn to mean anything more than being given the opportunity to make a fresh start in life.

But opportunity needs to be used.

The opportunity I had been given was to ask questions; the more the better. I needed to question my every habit, belief, attitude, like and dislike: in short, everything.

When I had questioned and worked out *for myself* what I believed to be true and what I believed to be false I needed to go further still. I needed to dare to journey into virgin territory, to live a new life of exploration and adventure in the world of the Spirit.

But that was in the future, I thought.

My most pressing need was to rid myself of the massive resentment I had built up against my parents, whether or not I continued in an active relationship with them.

Curiously, as I became aware of the need to review my feelings towards my parents I became aware also of disliking myself for disliking them. Something, somewhere, was wrong. And yet, as much as I tried, I just could not work out what.

I had yet to learn that any life changing insight is a gift of God.

(3)

Around this time I bought a copy of the well known prayer credited to St. Francis of Assisi. You probably know the one I mean:

"Lord, make me an instrument of your peace.

Where there is hatred, let me sow love;

where there is injury, pardon;

where there is doubt, faith;

where there is despair, hope;

where there is darkness, light;

where there is sadness, joy.

Divine Master, grant that I may

not so much seek

to be consoled, as to console;

to be understood, as to understand;

to be loved, as to love.

For

it is in giving that we receive;

it is in pardoning that we are pardoned;

it is in dying that we are born to eternal life."

I lingered for a long time over the penultimate line: "it is in pardoning that we are pardoned." Somehow, in a way I could not properly grasp, it seemed to explain why I was so confused. Then came a thud which could have been that of a penny dropping: perhaps I had not been pardoned because I had not pardoned my parents.

That was it. I was on my way!

My rejoicing was short lived. It soon became apparent that what St. Francis meant by pardoning was a pardoning from the heart. I could say, "I forgive you Mum; I forgive you Dad," until I was blue in the face and achieve precisely nothing. I would be mouthing the right words, but they would be the words of a pious parrot.

The conclusion I arrived at was sound. As I was soon to discover, true forgiveness arises from an inner depth where hurt does not rule; that is, from the kingdom of God within.

(At this point you may care to read in Luke's Gospel, 5.17-26, the story of Jesus healing a paralytic and forgiving him his sins. Dwell for a while, if you will, on verse 23: "Which is easier: to say, 'Your sins are forgiven,' or to say, 'Get up and walk'?" How do you answer?)

To continue: with thought I had illuminated the problem, but this was as far as thought took me; which was no distance at all from a still real and present danger of returning to drinking.

There came then my experience of the Divine Presence as complete and as beautiful as the first. It happened late one Thursday evening. I had been given a lift home from an AA meeting by another alcoholic, Dick, and his wife, Julie. She had been to an Al-Anon meeting (Al-Anon caters for the needs of relatives and friends of alcoholics). As was their habit, they stayed for a couple of cups of coffee and a natter about nothing in particular. It was all very pleasant.

After Dick and Julie left I settled down to watch an hour long television drama in the *Thriller* (?) series, another part of my Thursday evening routine at that time. I was completely absorbed in the unfolding story when, abruptly, I became aware of a change within me and in the air around me, then of *The Presence*. I had had a number of similar experiences between the very first one and that evening in the Fall of 1980, but none so intense or beautiful as this. Not for the first time tears flowed freely down my cheeks. They were silent tears, but tears of what?

Tears of happiness? Tears of joy? Of recognition? Of under-standing? I don't know. I honestly don't know. All I can say is that they were a spontaneous response to an indescribably beautiful moment of peace and oneness. It was as if I were being embraced by Love itself.

Returned to a normal condition I sat quietly for a while and tried to recall all that had happened. Then I went to bed.

It was not until I woke up the next morning and was getting ready for work that I recognized the change in me: I no longer felt resentment, anger, or any other negative emotion towards my parents. The same was true of my feelings about everyone else whose influence on me I had seen fit to curse.

Let me be quite clear about this. My memory had not been wiped clean; rather my perception of it had been transformed. Its images were clearer and stood in a radically different relation to one another.

Nor was I free of pain. That was still there, doing its work. So were my many doubts and uncertainties. But! The resentments, the anger, the bitterness and the hatred which, in lethal concert, had threatened to destroy me, were gone.

A further and no less valuable outcome of this experience was my recognition of a dazzlingly obvious truth: if I was to a very large extent the product of the various forces at play in the environment in which I had grown up, so my parents were to an equally large extent the product of theirs.

And what was true of them and of me was true for everyone. Without exception.

It was a truth that changed my life.

It changed my life, not simply because I recognized it as a truth, but because it sank from my head to my heart to become an essential part of my very being.

*

I should perhaps add a little footnote to this story. In celebration of being given so important an understanding I framed an A4 copy of the St. Francis prayer and gave it to my parents. It remained on a dressing table in their bedroom until my mother entered a nursing home in 1989.

(4)

Much of what I have said about the conditioning to which we are all subject may read as though copied verbatim from a book on DIY psychology. You may have been also reminded of Pavlov and his dogs. There is in fact nothing new in what I have said. It is perhaps true to say that nothing new has been said on the subject for several thousands of years. Moses said it all well before Pavlov, Freud, Jung, Adler, you and me were twinkles in our fathers' eyes.

If you turn to the book of Exodus (20.5) you will find a well-known passage in which God is reported to have said to Moses: "I, the Lord your God, am a jealous God, punishing the children for the sin of the fathers to the third and fourth generation of those who hate me..."

At a first reading you can be forgiven for understanding these words to be those of a vindictive God, a tyrant to be feared, rather than a Creator to be loved. Is this not often the case in the Old Testament? However, before we dismiss them so peremptorily I think they deserve a more considered look, bearing in mind the time and the circumstances in which they were set. Is it not likely that if a second Moses were to deliver the same message today he would use very different language? Can we, for instance, imagine this latter-day Moses describing God as a jealous God? And would it not be more incredible still were he even to consider the possibility of HE WHO IS punishing children for the faults of their parents?

So, where does this leave us?

Can we not, dare we not, go further and reject without the slightest reservation the idea that what Moses described as punishment is anything of the kind? May we not see it rather as the working out of an inevitable consequence; the harvest reaped from the sowing of ill chosen seeds? Consider: is it not quite inevitable that the effects of the faults of parents - most of which are not wrongs, as such, but the products of ignorance - will be felt not only by their children but by their grandchildren and great grandchildren, or even by those at a further remove?

From this we can see that by the time we first claim to have a mind of our own and begin to insist that we're quite capable of thinking for ourselves, thank you very much, we are, in truth, thinking with minds conditioned by the million and one influences to which we have been subject since birth. Here is a problem common to us all: unless we happen to have been born to perfect parents, to have been brought up among perfect relations and perfect friends in a perfect environment, and to have been educated by perfect teachers in perfect schools. Who would wish such a dismal fate on anyone?

This is all on the downside of what Moses had to say. There is a very substantial upside. If you dig just a little deeper into Moses' thinking it soon becomes apparent just how shrewd a man he was. It could even be argued that he inspired Jesus' teaching about the need to be born again if we would enter the kingdom of God.

An example may be found in Leviticus (26.39-42): "Those of you who are left will waste away in the lands of their enemies because of their sins; also because of their fathers' sins they will waste away. But if they will confess their sins and the sins of their fathers - their treachery against me and their hostility towards me... I will remember my covenant with Jacob and my covenant with Isaac and my covenant with Abraham..."

Again: "But if they will confess their sins and the sins of their fathers..."

Take a pause, if you will, for here is something to ponder; to ponder slowly and carefully; deeply and well. (You may find it useful first to read the whole of Chapter 26 in Leviticus.) Could it be that Moses is telling us exactly the same as he told his countrymen: namely, that if we recognize where our fathers (and mothers, grandfathers, grandmothers, uncle Tom Cobley and all) were mistaken, and do not repeat their errors, but, rather, do what we truly understand and believe to be right in the light of our own experience and deep consideration, then all shall be well, and all manner of things shall be well?

I believe so.

(5)

The openings, or insights, I had as the direct result of a few moments in front of a television set may be summarized briefly.

We can do no other than to wander the paths directed by our conditioning until such time as we are led to question what it is that motivates us. Jesus calls this process being born from above, or being born again.

That said, there are probably any number of ways of arriving at the moment of this second birth. I cannot recommend alcoholism to you as one to be sought.

It needs always to be remembered that a second birth is only a beginning. Every last part of my experience, however small, only strengthens this truth. I know I can allow no attitude, no habit, not the least part of my behavior, to be exempt from the possibility of challenge and change. Whatever is inconsistent with the free flow of the Life in the Spirit must go. It's as simple and as difficult as that.

Many are the questions that need to be asked.

But questions beget answers.

And answers need to be understood to be of any use.

What I came to understand in this particular case has to do

with a great deal more than forgiveness.

Above all, I saw not only that the ability to forgive is rather a gift of God than an act of will, but that all life changing openings are gifts of God.

(6)

. I can understand now why Jesus returns so often to the subject of forgiveness. He recognizes the spirit of forgiveness as essential to spiritual development. He is also aware that the one who forgives can gain far more than the one who is forgiven, which is probably why he said, "Forgive, and you will be forgiven. Give, and it will be given to you. A good measure, pressed down, shaken together and running over, will be poured into your lap. For with the measure you use, it will be measured to you."

(7)

To forgive can bring about a complete healing. It can heal the one who forgives and the one who is forgiven; the "sinner" and the one who is "sinned" against; and it can create harmony where once was discord.

Can.

But can is a possibility, not a certainty; for it is, I have learned, a sad truth that forgiveness on its own is not always sufficient to heal old wounds. Sometimes these wounds are too deep and have festered for too long to be so easily removed.

The wisdom of Moses should alert us to the great and ever present danger inherent in this situation: infection. Wounds of the soul are among the most infectious of human sufferings; the most difficult to diagnose accurately; the most difficult to cure.

It is time for specifics.

By the grace of God - and I do mean by the grace of God; I can claim no credit for myself - I was enabled to forgive my parents the mistakes I believed, and still believe, they made in my upbringing. I was enabled to forgive my sixth form classmates the wounds they inflicted on me; Kate too; and, at a later date, in a different context, Jenny. I was even enabled to forgive myself for the ways in which I had consciously contributed to my own hurt.

It was a good start, but the wounds were still there. They still limited the development of my potential as a human being in that they denied God's love the opportunity of finding in my life the expression it sought, and still seeks.

(8)

My encounter with Pastor M brought into the light much of what I have shared with you. For this I am grateful. He provided me with the key to the hitherto impregnable door which stood between me and freedom. Had I had the vision and the courage to use this key I would have advanced immeasurably the healing of my soul. Of that I am sure. But I did not. I chose instead to settle for what I had been already given, which was, by any standard, a great deal.

It was not a good decision. All it achieved - but even that I did not see at the time - was to expose my lack of faith in the God who had been so consistently faithful to me. It also exposed my ignorance of God's generosity, which truly has no limits.

There is a lesson to be learned here.

Until the breakdown of my relationship with Jenny in the Fall of 1981 - which led to my meeting with Pastor M - I had, for the best part of a year, been happier and more contented than at any time in my life. I was too contented. I neglected one of the essentials of the Spirit led life and the program of recovery of AA, which, for the alcoholic, are synonymous. Instead of periodically pressing the pause button and taking stock of what I was doing, thinking and feeling I allowed the glitz of my enjoyment of the passing days to blind me. I was rested on my laurels; or I would have been had they not been an illusion. Their actual comfort was the comfort of a bed of nails.

When the blow fell and Jenny rejected me in favor of her former lover the pain I experienced was a familiar pain. It was one to which I had become accustomed; one that had the habit of returning every so often. My sixth form classmates had rejected me. Kate had rejected me, then medical school and my first and second wives. There were also the several employers who had seen fit to dispense with my services over the years.

Could I not say that life had rejected me?

That is what I truly believed; deep, deep, deep down in the darkest and murkiest reaches of my being. It was a delusion I accepted as a truth not to be questioned; one whose tentacles reached everywhere to do their malign worst. In secret they wrought all kinds of havoc, and had for a very long time.

So, in the Fall of 1981, when I screamed at Pastor M, "But that's too good for me," I verbalized a belief that, in secret, had dominated much of my life. Still I refused to hold this ridiculous belief in the one Light that would have enabled me to see it for what it was and to turn it to good use.

I dared not to hold it in that Light.

Fear held me back.

(How clear are the eyes of hindsight!)

Had I seen that belief for what it was, had I allowed that Light to illumine my way forward, I should have been obliged to navigate the boundless waters of Freedom and, in so doing, to live a totally new life.

The prospect terrified me.

There was nothing new in this fear. It was one I had recognized and admitted to for a long time; but I had never tried to understand it, never tried to overcome it.

I understand now.

The overcoming? Time and life will provide the commentary.

It is perhaps appropriate here to quote a few lines from the latter part of Francis Thompson's wonderful poem, *The Hound of Heaven:*

"Whom wilt thou find to love ignoble thee,
Save Me, save only Me?
All which I took from thee I did but take,
Not for thy harms,
But just that thou might'st seek it in My arms.
All which thy child's mistake
Fancies as lost, I have stored for thee at home:
Rise, clasp My hand, and come.

"Halts by me that footfall:
Is my gloom, after all,
Shade of His hand, outstretched caressingly?
'Ah, fondest, blindest, weakest,
I am He whom thou seekest!'"

Perhaps you take the point.

(9)

A brief aside.

The more thought I give to my encounter with Pastor M the more I feel myself to be looking at my sickness, my alcoholism, in a completely fresh light. I see it less as the twisted bundle of emotional and psychological problems I have long believed it to be than as a sickness, a cramping, a constriction, of the soul. This is not to say that my behavior and attitude did not - and to some extent still do - give evidence of emotional and psychological problems. They most certainly did, and occasionally still do. But evidence, in this instance sometimes spectacular evidence, can be more apparent than real. In truth, it may be no more than a pointer to a far more subtle problem to be found at the very core of our being.

I believe it to be true here.

I believe it to be true in much sickness.

There, at the very core of our being, may be found the source of the power that governs not only our behavior but our whole personality.

(10)

More contributed to the sense of unworthiness I expressed with such passion to Pastor M than the harm I had suffered. I was becoming increasingly aware of the harm done by me to a long procession of innocents, a column headed by my first wife and our four children.

It was a considerable harm, much of which is apparent to this day. I do not, however, believe I should dwell on it. This is not because I see the harm I have done as a mite less important than the harm done to me, but because I feel it would invade the private worlds of those I love, or for whom I care a great deal. Their hurt is not mine to share.

Although when I met Pastor M I was aware of having been an instrument of suffering I had not then tried to assess the harm I had done. I lacked the courage. It's as simple as that.

The truth is, I have never sat down and made a conscious effort at such an assessment. I'm glad I have not, for I doubt if I could cope with the flood of remorse that would follow in its wake.

In any case the working of time has been more merciful. It has opened to me a greater knowledge and understanding of who I have wronged, and how, than any amount of conscious effort.

A greater knowledge.

Let me emphasize the "greater".

I doubt if it ever will be complete.

(11)

The priceless gift of being enabled to forgive my parents and others the wounds they inflicted on me soothed those wounds. It did not by any means heal them, nor did it take from them their power to limit my growth.

Similarly, although after a further interval I was able to accept that God had forgiven me for the harm I had done; and, eventually, was enabled to forgive myself, many of the wounds I had inflicted on others were still all too visible. I saw them, I could feel the pain they caused and, thank God, I shared that pain.

I still do.

I hope to continue in sharing that pain until such time as those I have hurt may be enabled to forgive me.

May be enabled.

There is no certainty in "may".

There is a certainty in forgiveness. Its name is healing.

*

Let me take another trip around the circuit and look again at my own experience to see what more may be learned from it. I do this in the firm belief that the lessons to be learned from experience are almost without number, and that what is true for me is likely to be true for you.

I have spoken of being enabled to forgive my parents, but that is not what actually happened. I was, rather, enabled to see in my upbringing the failings in theirs, and that the three of us were, equally, victims of the ignorance of countless generations of our ancestors.

Without this understanding I doubt if I could ever have forgiven my parents their mistakes; with it I could do no other. Today, what at that time I called forgiveness, I can regard as nothing less than an act of union; the great and ugly barrier of ignorance which had stood for so long between me and my parents was no more.

But the understanding came first.

And the understanding and the forgiveness born of it were gifts of God. I was too blinded by the pains of anger and resentment and bitterness, too sick, ever to have seen the truth for myself.

(12)

A gift of God.

You can't really expect a gift of God to be comparable with gifts of the sort we exchange at Christmas, now can you? A gift of God has to be something really special.

And so it is.

When someone gives you a present at Christmas you can, if you so choose, unwrap it, show it to no one, and get your pleasure or use from it in total privacy.

A gift of God is very different. For one thing, it doesn't come in a parcel; for another, although we may give it a particular name - such as understanding, forgiveness, patience, joy - it is, in all essentials, always the same gift: love.

A gift that comes in a parcel can be lifted from its parcel and examined. We cannot put our hands on a gift of God; we cannot see it, or smell it, or taste it. It cannot be bought; it cannot be sold. It cannot be possessed, for there is no ownership in the kingdom of Heaven; there are no rights of exclusive use.

And yet gifts of God transform lives; they give Life.

How?

By giving them away, by passing them on, by becoming channels through which God's great gift of love flows and is multiplied; by offering ourselves in every way we can as witnesses to the healing power of this love.

God's love heals, that is for sure, but, if my own experience is a true reflection of a generality, it also makes us aware of pain and all forms of suffering. It can be said to guarantee us a share in that pain and suffering.

Can we know the love and peace of God except through suffering? Can we rise above suffering except by suffering? I doubt it.

But neither do I doubt that the gift of God's love has the power to release us from bondage to the source of our suffering, if we grant it free passage; if, after receiving it, we give it away.

Let me close this chapter and make ready for the next by offering you a belief and a prayer.

Truly to understand is to forgive; to forgive is to love as Christ loves; to love as Christ loves is Life.

Lord, I beg you, grant me understanding.

Chapter 5

A work of fiction has a beginning, a middle and an end. It has a plot and characters. The actions of these characters; their relationships with one another; their responses to the circumstances imposed on them by the author; all are designed to move the plot along to a satisfying and, hopefully, not too predictable conclusion.

A work of non-fiction which has as an essential part of its subject matter the author, the plot of whose life is yet to be worked out in full, cannot follow so neat a pattern. Nor is it as easy or, perhaps, even possible for the author to take the same detached view of his subject as can the creator of fiction.

There, contained within two short paragraphs, is the substance of the difficulty I faced as I contemplated this final chapter: what to say in order to bring the whole thing to a neat end?

With the best will in the world I must doubt if it can be done.

My life, like yours, is still in transit. But to where? And to what? If there is a where and a what, that is. But whether or not there is a where and/or a what, a life in transit is a life in motion. Any kind of motion, be it from one place to another, from one time to another, from one condition to another, requires the action of some kind of force. Unless that action is motiveless, and probably very few are, we have a plot: do we not?

Problem!

We are talking here of real lives: my life and yours. We have a vested interest in the plot and its ending. Is it to be happy or tragic? Is it predictable? Will it be satisfying? Will there, in truth, be an end? Or will its apparent end be no more than the prelude to a sequel, *Life: the Next Dimension*?

So, given we have a plot that is still unfolding, we must have an author. Agreed?

We are making progress.

Let us not, though, lose sight of the fact that the unfolding plot is the plot of a real life, not a work of fiction.

Provided I have spoken truthfully of my experiences and the understanding I have gleaned from them, then, in writing this book, I have acted rather in the capacity of a reporter than an author; albeit a reporter who is the subject of his own reporting!

I feel it is important to make this distinction. A reporter reports; an author of fiction creates.

I did not create my life any more than you created yours, or not in the sense that we might be said to have brought ourselves into being. Clearly we did not.

Then again, the sculptor does not create the stone he shapes into a beautiful form we may all admire, nor the potter his clay. Even so, from the materials available to them, they both create objects of beauty.

The material we are given to shape into something beautiful is more precious by far than stone or clay. It is life. But, whereas the work of the sculptor and potter has a visible end in a fixed form, our material refuses to solidify. It is always in motion. We can never say, "This is me. There is no more to be done. I am finished. Look and admire."

There is another difference between us and the sculptor and potter. They start work on virgin material. By the time we realize we need to start work on the material we have been given - life! - others have already started shaping it on our behalf, a subject we addressed in previous chapters.

We are in the position of a novelist compelled to finish a story started by someone else. This is no easy task, especially as we cannot simply erase the other's work.

It may or may not be a cause for regret that we do not share with the novelist his ability to go back to page one and rewrite the whole of our lives' stories. We could then edit out the harm we have done and write in the good we did not do.

On the other hand we might wish that God had created us so that our lives resembled those lived by Rupert Bear and his friends: Billy Badger, Algy Pug, Edward Trunk, Willy Mouse, Pong Ping and Tiger Lily. Rupert, bless him - I love him dearly - has a wonderful life. Adventure follows upon adventure, day in, day out, year in, year out, without anyone ever coming to any lasting harm. At the end of each day's adventuring he returns to his home in Nutwood there to sleep safe and snug in his own bed.

Rupert doesn't even have to grow up. Why should he? Where is his need? His creator looks after him through every moment of his life, be he asleep or be he awake. Suffering, real suffering, does not exist in his world.

I have to admit to a certain envy of Rupert. He has a great and adventurous life laid on for him. He knows nothing of poverty and pain; enjoys perfect security within and without a loving home; and he has friends galore, with whom he never quarrels.

It is also true to say that as a consequence of not being allowed by his creator to grow up Rupert is, and always will be, his plaything. But does this matter if he enjoys the life he is given, which he clearly does?

It might be as well if we remind ourselves that Rupert is a creature of fiction. Apart from his creator he can do nothing; nor can he as much as dream of doing anything, or refuse the smallest thing required of him by his creator.

No, on further thought I do not envy Rupert his life; his life is a fiction, an illusion. He exists only in the mind of his creator and those who, like me, enjoy sharing for a while his creator's fantasies. Yet, in common with the sculpture and the pot; in common with any expression of the human imagination, be it in the field of music, art, literature or what-have-you, there is contained within the adventures of Rupert a reality, which is a part at least of the essence of his creator.

The same, I believe, is true of us: without exception there resides in each one of us a part at least of the essence of our

Creator.

Here the likeness ends.

Abruptly.

It ends because a part of the essence of our Creator, God, which resides in us is consciousness.

Rupert is aware neither of himself nor his creator. The same is true of Leonardo's *Mona Lisa* and the couple embracing in Rodin's *The Kiss*. Magnificent works of art, yes, but conscious of themselves or their creator they are not.

The gap between ourselves and Rupert widens further when we become aware of wants and needs, likes and dislikes, love and hate and all of the million and one conflicts we may experience. Rupert knows none of these things. But, then, we have been given life, real life, not an illusion of life, and we are able to do with it as we will.

Or can we?

This seems to be a good point to recapitulate a theme recurrent throughout this book.

As we become aware of our abilities we are free to use them only to the extent to which that freedom has not been affected by the many conditioning factors at work in the environment in which we were born and grew up. These factors can and do inhibit or enhance our abilities and our perception of them. Could this perhaps be a reason why our Creator, our God, visits us at various stages in our lives to remind us in often pointed fashion of Himself? He does this even if, prior to these visits, we would deny His very existence.

There is in this assertion a very positive statement, but it is a statement based on personal experience. Working on the principle that in their essential nature my own experiences are unlikely to be substantially different from those of anyone else then the same is probably true for you. To put it quite plainly: you will almost certainly have been visited by God on several occasions in your life. Whether or not you recognized His presence is quite another matter; and it is another matter again to recognize His presence and to respond to it.

(2)

Let me yet again quote from personal experience.

When I was admitted to the Maudsley psychiatric hospital on Denmark Hill in south-east London as my University career came to its inevitable end I was a very sick young man. A part of this sickness manifested itself in violence. At frequent intervals I would wreck everything in sight and attack anyone who attempted to stop me. As a consequence I spent most my time locked in a single room of the refractory ward, the Villa.

The male nurses rarely entered my room when I started throwing its few furnishings about and smashing the glass in its two doors. They were normally, and understandably, content to wait until I ran out of steam.

One day I was not left to run out of steam; nor was I overwhelmed by a squad of male nurses. Ridiculously - and in the circumstances it was quite ridiculous - a solitary female staff nurse normally employed on the women's section of the Villa came into my room. She had her hands held open, palms upwards, and they extended towards me. There was in her eyes and on her face no trace of fear or anxiety. Absolutely none. Instead, there was about her an aura of the utmost tranquility. I had never encountered anything like it; nor have I since.

The uniqueness of Staff Nurse Elizabeth Mary Grace's approach disarmed totally the forces of anarchic violence raging within me. I could do no other than allow her to take my hands and guide me to my bed, where we sat side by side, my hands still enclosed in hers. I cannot remember what she said to me or how I replied to her, but I do remember quite clearly how much at peace I felt, and how safe. Most of all I remember feeling safe.

We talked on a good number of occasions after that, many of

them when I was not disturbed. I learned that Nurse Grace was a devout Catholic, due in the not too distant future to take the veil. She even shared with me the substance of her faith, and I listened.

Intently.

Had I been able to know Nurse Grace for a little while longer I might have been able to grasp and accept the idea that Jesus came not to make the good feel better but "to seek and to save what was lost" (Luke 19.10). In the event, she went home to Ireland for a fortnight's holiday and in that time I was transferred to another hospital.

I have never forgotten Nurse Grace: her love, her tranquility, her faith, her simplicity and her devotion to Jesus and to living the life she believed he wanted her to live. I never forgot her in the very worst of my drinking days, except that during that time she and the Jesus she loved so dearly were to me no more than elusive, hopeless, longings.

Even so, God had made Himself known to me through Nurse Grace.

(3)

We need now to jump from the 50s to 1968. I was married and had fathered four children, but done little else that may be regarded as constructive. I had drifted in and out of work without any sense of purpose whatsoever. My family life lacked direction too. Although in my own peculiar way I loved my wife and children, it was not a way that looked to creating a home worth living in or to giving my children a childhood they would be able to look back on with affection as golden years. Sadly for all of us I just kept on drifting, empty and aching, concerning myself only with getting through each day with the least possible struggle.

Quite often I drank too much, but I thought of my drinking as fun, a means of relieving the monotony of everyday existence, not as a problem. Until near the end of this period it was very much a private pleasure. I shared it with no one, for I drank when I should have been working the territory I covered as a sales representative.

After a while the drinking I kept as a private pleasure was joined by increasingly bizarre and often downright dangerous behavior, but this I chose to overlook. Then I knocked a woman from her bicycle. I did not kill her, thank God, or cause her any serious physical harm. I can only hope she suffered no lasting psychological damage.

Quite properly I lost my driving license and my job. For the first time I became aware of being a little boy lost with nowhere to go and nothing to do. I truly was a little boy lost. At the age of 33 I felt like a child of 10 compelled to live in an adult world.

I should not like to estimate how often my mind returned in envy to Nurse Grace. She had had something to which she was willing to devote her all; I had nothing. (In my reckoning of the time a wife and four children didn't count.) Worse, I did not have the faintest idea of why I had nothing.

It was then that God chose to pay me another visit, this time in the perhaps unlikely shape of a couple of Jehovah's Witnesses. I listened to what they had to say on the doorstep and then, because they quite obviously believed in what they were saying, invited them in.

As a result of this introductory session I was visited thereafter at weekly intervals for several weeks by a, presumably, more senior man. He opened up the Bible to me as no one else had even tried to do. Everything we read together, everything we discussed, fascinated me. Fascinated is truly the word. So irresistible was the attraction of that book I went out, avowed atheist and cynic though I was, and bought one for myself.

After a few weeks I grew tired of my tutor's attempts to interest me in becoming a Jehovah's Witness and asked him not to come back. He didn't. Even so, this was by no means the end of my interest in the Bible. I read the New Testament through from start to finish. Many were the passages I read and reread.

Much of what I read excited me as I had never before been excited. Why? Because I was reading about love, about hope, about faith, about purpose, about joy, about LIFE! LIFE spelt in capital letters: LIFE! LIFE!

I was right to be excited. We should shout the word from the rooftops, for that is what Jesus is all about: LIFE! LIFE IN ALL ITS RICHNESS AND SPLENDOR.

A peculiar few months followed. Although my initial enthusiasm did not last I could not get the idea out of my mind that in the Bible, in Jesus, I had found something of real value. I considered going to church, but never got round to it. For one thing, the memories I had of the hideously pious practices of religion I had witnessed in my childhood Sunday school days acted as a powerful deterrent; then there was the fear that my wife would think I had gone mad, or soft, or both. You see, I had come to understand from my reading of the Bible that religion was not something to be practiced only on Sunday, however simple or however splendid the surroundings. I had begun to question if anything I had been taught about Christianity was true. It seemed to me that religious practices were possibly the least important part of it; that it was surely something which had to be lived through every minute of every hour of every day.

God had visited me again, but I had not recognized him.

(4)

The possibilities I had had opened to me remained unexplored, part of an impossible dream. Hope slowly faded.

Then, in the spring of 1969, it was renewed in the oddest way.

One day I took time off from work. It was something I did with monotonous regularity. As was my habit when playing truant I drank several pints of beer over the lunch hour. Slightly drunk and very depressed, I happened to walk past the Quaker Meeting House in central Nottingham. My eyes fell on the sign outside, which announced a resident caretaker. I rang the bell.

I talked for a long time with the lady who was then the caretaker. As a result I attended my first Meeting for Worship on the following Sunday. To my great surprise I took to the largely silent, totally unprogrammed, hour of worship like a duck to water. I truly felt as though I had found my spiritual home.

At about this time my relationship with alcohol, which always had been open to question, reached a crisis point. My drinking started to spiral out of control.

This defied all reason. Having found my spiritual home, and time was to prove I had, what reason was there for me to set about destroying myself?

A fundamentalist would no doubt answer this question in simple terms: God was pointing me in the one direction; Satan tempting me to take the other - and succeeding. It is an explanation that combines the virtue of simplicity with a fair degree of accuracy. The old metaphors have much to commend them.

The fact is, I was a damaged personality newly aware of being damaged, however vague that awareness. I had been given a glimpse, via my Jehovah's Witness friend, the Bible and, latterly, the Quaker Meeting for Worship, of the possibility of being healed. Nowhere was this more obvious than in the Meeting for Worship. That was a revelation.

But!

I was a damaged personality – about that there could be no doubt - and so damaged that I perceived my fellow worshipers to be without weakness or fault. This was nonsense, of course, yet another symptom of how damaged I was, but to me it was a truth.

I drew comparisons. Envy, malice and all manner of unjust thoughts and accusations promptly erupted from the darkness enveloping my soul. The people with whom I joined in worship and to whom, in that magic hour, I felt so close, became strangers to be feared outside of the Meeting Room. They all had their lives organized. They were happy, well off, had good jobs and friends, and interests about which I could only dream. They looked out on their worlds with confidence; all their doubts, if they had ever had any, were behind them.

They and I had absolutely nothing in common.

My drinking worsened. Reality and I met rarely, and then only when it could not be avoided. To have been consistent with the resentments and the anger and envy boiling inside me I should have stopped attending Meetings for Worship. I did not. I missed very few Meetings, and then only because I had 'flu or some other "legitimate" bug. Alcohol was never the cause.

Astonishing.

My drinking continued in its downwards spiral. Reality and I parted company altogether, or, rather, my inability to recognize the Ultimate Reality at work in my life kept me apart from that Reality and made foreign the lesser realities of everyday life.

Until, that is, one Saturday morning in the April of 1977.

(5)

Before I move on to bring to an end this final chapter I feel I should share with you a few thoughts on the value of sharing: that is, on the value of sharing with others not from what we have, though that has its place, but from what we are. I would also ask you to consider that "what we are" might better be stated as "what we have become".

To open our hearts and minds in sharing with others is no small thing. It calls for courage, faith and love; for often we are called upon not to share our knowledge and our strengths, but to expose our vulnerability and pain. Did Jesus not say, "If anyone wants to be a follower of mine, let him renounce himself and take up his cross every day and follow me. Anyone who wants to save his life will lose it; but anyone who loses his life for my sake, will save it" (Luke 9.23,24 NJB)?

Look at these words, please, in the light of our consideration of the value of sharing. Do we not in effect renounce ourselves (or our Selves) when we share with another our vulnerability and pain? I believe we do, because one of the things we do when we share is to destroy false images of ourselves, most commonly of our own creation. The cross we must then take up each and every day is the cross of being known to others *and to ourselves* as the person we have become.

That we know ourselves (or our Selves) is crucial. This I cannot emphasize too strongly, for this is the truth of the cross we carry as we follow Jesus.

"Anyone who wants to save his life will lose it..." We come back to the same thing, don't we? If we try consciously to create and preserve an image of ourselves, usually one that radiates only our virtues, do we not rapidly lose all contact with the reality hidden by that image? Does it not also suggest that we may be afraid of who and what we truly are?

"... but anyone who loses his life for my sake, will save it." This turns the last paragraph inside out. If we get rid of the image with courage, with faith, with love, then what we are left with is the reality of ourselves as we truly are. And that is nothing less than children of God.

We carry our cross of truth. Image, that false idol, dies on it. What is saved, what is resurrected, is Reality.

We can also think of Paul's second letter to the Corinthians when he wrote (2 Cor 12:9) that God had told him, "My grace is sufficient for you, for my power is made perfect in weakness." And then in the next verse he wrote of himself, "For when I am weak, then I am strong."

Relate both of these sentences, if you will, to the explosion in recent years of the number of successful self-help groups in existence. AA was the first. It took off in 1935 when a couple of alcoholics discovered that by sharing their experiences, strengths and hopes with one another they were able to stay away from alcohol. More than that, they began to live in the fullest possible sense of the word.

It has been my good fortune to be a part of AA and to need to learn to share freely and openly my experiences, strengths, hopes, vulnerability and pain with other alcoholics, male and female. I needed also to learn to listen with an uncritical and non-judgmental heart to what others have shared with me, often things they had thought they would never be able to tell anyone.

Whatever the direction of the sharing it has always had value. I anticipate no difference in the future. That I can say this with confidence is because everything I have experienced witnesses to the fact that whenever truth is shared, and never more so than when it is the truth of the human heart, God is always present.

Always.

Without exception.

Remember, too, what Jesus told a Pharisee who invited him to dinner: "Did not the one who made the outside make the inside also? But give what is inside (the dish) to the poor, and everything will be clean for you" (Luke 11.40,41).

I wonder if in saying this Jesus had in mind the kind of giving, or sharing, we have been discussing?

(6)

It has been my aim in writing this book to speak accurately of relevant parts of my total experience; my understanding of those parts; and, finally, how I arrived at that understanding. I need now to remember that my understanding is only the understanding of the present moment. It will change, and as it changes so shall I. May it be so for you!

This means, of course, that it is quite impossible for me to bring my labors to a neat end. Were I writing a novel this would probably be undesirable. But I am not writing a novel; I am writing a book dealing with some of the more significant moments and periods of a life still in transit. Neatness has not been one of its more prominent features.

I am conscious of changes within myself since I first put finger to keyboard, and this is good; it is a product of my original purpose. What was most definitely *not* on the menu was a search for a set of beliefs upon which I could plant my flag and there make a stand against all comers including, probably, truth.

It would have been suicide.

At best I should have been making for myself a spiritual straitjacket, for whether we like it or not change, like the poor, will always be with us.

Change.

If this book is nothing else it is an account of change.

The most important changes of which I am aware have been those relating to my inner life; that is, to my relationship with God through Jesus; to my relationships with other people; and to my relationship with myself.

Echoes here, I think, of, "Love the Lord your God with all your heart and with all your soul and with all your mind... Love your neighbor as yourself" (Matt 22.37-40).

I cannot help but also call to mind a small part of the wisdom of dear Brother Lawrence of the pots and pans: "We must know before we love, and to know God we must often think of Him."

So, let me try to draw a sketch of these changes, a brief route map of how my faith has arrived where it is now, albeit a faith still in motion.

(7)

Sunday school and adolescence turned me implacably against religion. It would have been surprising had they not, for the religion I was taught was a religion that could be learned, rather like multiplication tables and the basic rules of grammar. This you do, that you don't; this is right, that is wrong; this is good, that is bad. The reward of the good was eternal life in heaven; the punishment of the bad everlasting torment in hell. Emotions, motives, social pressures, these counted for nothing. It was the deed, being good and being seen to be good, that mattered.

Horrible!

Then, after the pit had opened beneath my feet I met Nurse Grace, which was to meet love in action. I cannot remember her once telling me I must or must not do anything; that I must think this or that. She didn't even try to tell me that God loved me, or that I should open my heart to Jesus. She did express the hope that one day I would know God.

I have already shared with you how Nurse Grace spoke to me about her faith without any trace of goody-goodiness. This and her simple sincerity impressed me more than anything she actually said; for when she spoke of Jesus she spoke not of an incredibly distant, austere and unreal figure, but of an active, actual, friend she loved with all her heart and all her soul and all her mind.

Nurse Grace sowed a seed. She was an agent of change.

My Jehovah's Witness friend was another agent. He introduced me to the riches contained within the Bible.

The Bible exposed to my startled gaze, as nothing else had, my emptiness. When I recognized this for what it was I began to feel a hunger. This was good, for the longer term. Within the Quaker Meeting for Worship I came to believe in the existence of God. Sort of. It was not a belief that changed my life, rather a feeble intellectual acknowledgment of the probability of His reality. I didn't know Him and, because I didn't know Him, I didn't love Him.

What can I say about Jesus? He certainly fascinated me. That much is undeniable. But it was a fascination that put him on the outside of everyday life. This Jesus could only be approached by

Saints, actual or apprentice, and I was neither.

The result was that my view of God, of Jesus, of the workings of the Spirit, was a distant one, unreal and dreamlike.

Eventually even that disappeared.

Then, in a few moments on a never to be forgotten morning, God became Reality and Jesus Christ the very incarnation of God. Now, comfortably more than 30 years on, God is still Reality and Jesus Christ the very incarnation of God. That is not to say my relationship with the Divine fossilized in the moment it assumed reality. It assuredly did not. It began, and continues, as a live relationship, a relationship in motion.

Long may it so remain.

In its early days, which were the early days of my recovery from alcoholism, I was aware of God only as He had been incarnate in Jesus Christ. I could relate better to an historic figure. It is probably true to say that my first conscious thought every morning was of Jesus. I don't mean by this that I woke up with one of the gospel stories about him on my mind, or that I immediately gave thought to one of his teachings. I didn't. That first thought was of Jesus the man. It could not be otherwise, for he was with me as a real Presence. True, I never saw him or heard his voice – I would have been somewhat alarmed if I had - but that in no way diminished his reality. He was with me when I woke up; he stayed with me all day. Wherever I went, whoever I met, whatever I did, I had Jesus as a constant and loving companion.

I had Jesus as a constant and loving companion, yes, but he was a silent companion, in every sense of the word. He never advised, guided or judged me. I never knew him to steer or to impel me in one direction or another.

Let me make a mistake, and I made them by the cartload, then I suffered the consequences.

If I failed to be truthful the stabbings of conscience made my life difficult to bear until I set the record straight as best I could, which was not often very well.

Let someone behave badly towards me and I had to respond in the best way I saw fit, which was only occasionally a good way.

Let me crave alcohol and I had to sweat it out.

I have no complaint about any part of this. After all, when a child is learning to walk - and I was a child in the gentle art of living - there comes the time when its parents must withhold their supporting hands.

To learn how to live without alcohol I had to sink the pride that had played so large a part in destroying me by listening to, and learning from, the experiences of other recovering alcoholics. I had to learn how to share openly with them from my own experiences. In this way I learned slowly, painfully slowly, how not to make quite so many mistakes. I learned, too, that I am not always obliged to respond when people behave badly towards me. Vitally, I learned that I did not need to be alone when I sweated out a craving for alcohol. Help was never more than a telephone call away.

I can see now that several things were happening here, nearly all of them at the very deepest levels of my being; several things, that is, in addition to the dawning of an awareness of just how ignorant I was in the art of living.

One of these "things" stands out way above the rest.

As day followed upon day I became more and more conscious of how much I was loved. I felt loved. This was not all. I felt myself to be in love and that Jesus was at the heart of this love. He was its source and its object. My condition made not a scrap of difference to him. Let me be in touch with reality or flying on cloud nine; let me be laughing or crying; breathing benevolence or spitting fire, still he loved me. I cannot say that my love for him was as consistent. It was not; nor is it still. Even so, I can perhaps claim that I was, and am, appreciably less inconsistent in this than in the other departments of my life. So powerful, so overwhelming, so consuming, was Jesus' presence that I never as much as dreamed of attempting to make a serious objective appraisal of the accounts of his earthly life as related in the Gospels of Matthew, Mark, Luke and John. I was far too wrapped up in *the* Gospel as it was being revealed to me to concern myself with bringing into question the truth, literal or otherwise, of what was written about Him. Which is the better: to read criticisms of the music of Bach, Beethoven, Haydn, Mozart or any of the other great composers, or to listen to it?

(8)

I was probably somewhere between six months and a year into recovery when I began truly to believe that it might be possible for me to live the rest of my life without resort to alcohol. The last whisperings of doubt ceased to trouble me. I was finding my feet, fumbling my way through the onset of spiritual adolescence. It was then another kind of doubt began to assail me. Had Jesus really been by my side all day, every day, for so long? Was it not more likely that what I thought of as *the* Greatest Reality had been, in truth, no more than a comforting fantasy, a psychological creation enabling me to survive a period fraught with all manner of dangers?

I questioned the gospels. No doubt there was a lot of truth and wisdom in them, but were they historically reliable documents? Never.

A different kind of thinking began to win control of my mind. Rational thought, reason, logic: these could be equated with sanity; and sanity had a very special appeal, in abundance.

There was then the miracle of 23 April 1977, for however hard I tried to describe it as something less than a miracle, I couldn't. Nor could I deny that I was still frequently aware of Jesus walking with me; silent as always, invisible and loving. This Jesus I loved, regardless of whether or not it made sense.

*

I was working at this time, struggling to cope with the demands of my first job since putting down the bottle. I was also taking the first steps towards leaving my parents' home - for the second time and at the age of 42! - and setting up one of my own. No sooner had I done this than I learned that my marriage was effectively ended. My wife, very understandably, was seeking a divorce. At much the same time my body began to remind me that I was a biologically normal man with normal male desires.

Without once taking pause to consider the wisdom of what I was about, willfully neglectful of AA advice not to embark on any new emotional entanglements in the first three years of recovery, I started on the way to sowing a few wild oats. It was an ambition which quickly led me into a disastrous second marriage to another alcoholic. Eighteen unhappy months later it was all over.

This experience gives rise to an obvious and frequently asked question: if Jesus was the friend I claimed him to be why did he, or God, or the Holy Spirit, not intervene to prevent a marriage doomed to failure? A lot of suffering, and not just my own, would have been avoided.

It would be very easy to answer this question in the language of punishment. The message to be heard was that God required from me a greater constancy of devotion, or else. This is a possibility but, frankly, I doubt very much if it gets within hooting distance of the truth.

I believe it to be far more likely that He did not intervene because He has no wish for any one of us to become old in body without being given the opportunity to mature in wisdom. I was not prevented from entering into a disastrous second marriage and from making many other painful mistakes because I believe God will, in no circumstances, take from me or from anyone else the freedom to choose as we will. This freedom to choose includes the freedom to make mistakes, even criminal mistakes, and to learn, or not, from them.

Please do not misunderstand me. I have in mind freedom as it is coupled and allied with learning and responsibility. License is nowhere in the frame. Choice has its consequences.

This I believe with all my heart and with all my soul and with all my strength and with all my mind, is the key to a faith that fuels the growth which ever reaches towards spiritual maturity and oneness with God. It is a faith founded in experiment and experience; in failure and in success; in grief and in bliss; in frustration and in fulfillment; in fantasy and in reality; in short, in the glorious gift of life.

(9)

I write about God loving me and about God acting through Jesus in the sure knowledge that God does love me and that, through Jesus, His influence on my life is profound.

Jesus is all important. He is the divine catalyst to whom I owe my all. He is the one who has brought to life in my life the love of God. No one can do more.

About the literal truth of the gospel accounts of Jesus' life I do not these days concern myself. Some passages are no doubt factual; some part fact, part fiction; some pure myth. It matters not to me which is what for a very simple reason: I have discovered that when I read the gospels I frequently enjoy the most extraordinary sensation of the words taking on a life of their own. In this life there are to be found none of the contradictions or inconsistencies of the printed word.

Let me say this again in a rather different way. The point I am trying to make is important. I use my intellect to understand the printed word. The Spirit lifts these same words from the printed page, parts them, and reveals to me an understanding beyond the reach of reason alone.

There is clearly a big difference in the means by which I arrive at these two forms of understanding. There is at least as big a difference in the use to which I put them.

Intellectual understanding is something I can call on when I need it. I can ignore it at will. Revealed understanding becomes at once a part of my deepest self, which may lie deeper even than my unconscious. I ignore it at my peril.

*

Let me now describe as best I can what does and does not happen when the words of a gospel lift off the page and take on a life of their own.

When I read a good novel every detail of the scene described by the author takes shape in my mind: I can visualize the setting and the faces, figures and dress of the characters involved; I can hear their voices, see their movements, get inside their minds.

This is seldom the case when I read a passage from the gospels. I can neither visualize the setting nor the faces, figures or dress of any of the participants, most especially of Jesus himself. Sometimes nothing more happens than this. I read, I struggle to make the best I can of the passage under my eyes, and that is it; end of story, no more.

At other times - and how precious these times are - the words become an irrelevance. They take on a life of their own. I feel a quickening of my heartbeat, a tension enters my breathing and, not infrequently, I experience a trembling in my limbs. This phase soon passes, to be followed by a great stillness of heart and mind and a quite undeniable sense of the Real Presence of God.

In these all too brief moments understanding of any kind is an irrelevance. The God whose Word I seek to understand and to live has me enfolded His arms.

Some time later, or it may be minutes or it may be days, I realize how much my understanding of the words I have read has changed, that my understanding has, in truth, become an ineradicable and beneficent part of me.

As a postscript to this section I should add that I have found it the most difficult to write. It is not easy to share something which, however much it means to me, might, and probably will, be regarded by some as symptomatic of a mental abnormality. With my history I must confess that this remains an area in which I am particularly sensitive.

There is, however, an overriding consideration: the need for all who have had experience of the healing power of the Holy Spirit to stand up and give witness to it. Should I continue to fail to do this, as I have largely failed thus far in my life, I do not fear for one moment that I will be punished by an avenging God. It is far more likely that I will, rather, deprive myself of the fulfillment speaking out will open to me. I shall have fallen at the post.

(10)

Think now, if you will, about growth; about growing up; about growing older.

Think about how, in this process, we first find our feet and start to become aware of the environment in which we live and the people who inhabit it and influence our behavior.

Think about how we become aware of our special talents and their scope, and of how we could use them to give to our lives a sense of direction and purpose.

Think about how we become aware of our limitations and the role these have in shaping our lives.

Think about how we make progress in our lives, if progress we make, and about how we respond to our various successes, failures and disappointments.

Is it not true that all of these things, and more, contribute to us acquiring our special sense of identity? It may also be argued that the more successful we are in life and in building a network of good social relationships as well as in our careers, the stronger is our sense of identity.

We know who we are. We may even believe we know our worth, or lack of it. We may even claim to "know ourselves".

*

Having given you so much to think about it is now a good time for us to look briefly at one of the most profound of Jesus' teachings. It is one to which I have referred before and is found in Luke's Gospel (9:23-25 NJB): "If anyone wants to be a follower of mine, let him renounce himself and take up his cross every day and follow me. Anyone who wants to save his life will lose it; but anyone who loses his life for my sake, will save it. What benefit is it to anyone to win the whole world and forfeit or lose his very self?"

So profound is this teaching it would reward a far longer and deeper consideration than I can presently give to it. I propose here only to look at one four word phrase within it: "let him renounce himself".

I believe the translators who labored to produce the New Jerusalem Bible served Jesus well when they chose to use *renounce* rather than the more common *deny*. That one word, *deny*, has possibly been responsible for more misunderstanding and unhappiness than any other in the whole of the scriptures. It has certainly done nothing to attract people to Christianity.

I had an uncle and an aunt, both lovely people, who once bought an expensive music center. It was a beautiful thing of which they were understandably proud, but they only ever played hymns on it. They believed, actually believed, that any other music was *denied* to them by Jesus Christ.

If we accept that "he must deny himself" is the best interpretation of what Jesus said we are faced with two possibilities. The first is that we should deny our own reality, which is a nonsense... isn't it?

The second possibility appears to make far more sense: we extend Jesus' words to read, "he must deny himself, *x, y or z*". For *x, y or z* you may substitute anything you enjoy doing.

My uncle and aunt chose to deny themselves the pleasures of exploring the universe that is music. Others have chosen to deny themselves the pleasures of the theater, dancing, laughter or a decent meal; many have failed to enjoy a healthy sex life because they have understood sex for pleasure, even with their spouse, to be sinful; many more dare not to share their innermost thoughts with anyone, because to do so they would have to reveal the truth of their "sinful" natures. I could go on. I will not. The tragedy is that many good people have been caught in this trap. Instead of enjoying the freedom promised by Jesus (see, for instance, Luke 4.18 and John 8.31,32) they have been imprisoned by the ignorance of their teachers.

If now we turn our thoughts to "let him *renounce* himself" it is possible at once to see one very big difference from "let him *deny* himself": it is very difficult, if not impossible, to add anything to it that makes any kind of sense. Who, for instance, would ever think of saying, "let him renounce himself the pleasures of the theater, or music, or sex"?

It is sufficient to stop, like Jesus, at "let him renounce himself". This brings us right back to our sense of identity; to how strong it is, or isn't; to the full impact of Jesus' "How blessed are the poor in spirit: the kingdom of Heaven is theirs" (Matt 5.3 NJB); and to the glorious self-revelation of his "I am the Way: I am Truth and Life" (John 14.6 NJB).

"He must renounce himself..."

Pause for a while on those four words. Consider them and what they might mean; what Jesus meant by them.

He does not say that if I would come after him I must give up food, or alcohol, or sex, or an evening at the theater or concert hall. He does not say I need to give up anything; anything, that is, except my very self. It is the demands of this self, the self I have so carefully cultivated and brought to maturity over many years; the self that is my individual persona, my ego, the sense of identity that separates me from everyone else, which I need to renounce totally. I need to renounce it so completely that it no longer exists.

Then, and only then, will I be able to follow without excess baggage in the Way that is Jesus and eventually discover for myself that he is Truth and Life.

Then I will not have grown up, I will have grown out. I will have grown out of myself and entered into that Life which is in and with Jesus, in God.

I look to that day.

May God bless you.

BOOKS

O is a symbol of the world, of oneness and unity. In different cultures it also means the "eye," symbolizing knowledge and insight. We aim to publish books that are accessible, constructive and that challenge accepted opinion, both that of academia and the "moral majority."

Our books are available in all good English language bookstores worldwide. If you don't see the book on the shelves ask the bookstore to order it for you, quoting the ISBN number and title. Alternatively you can order online (all major online retail sites carry our titles) or contact the distributor in the relevant country, listed on the copyright page.

See our website www.o-books.net for a full list of over 500 titles, growing by 100 a year.

And tune in to myspiritradio.com for our book review radio show, hosted by June-Elleni Laine, where you can listen to the authors discussing their books.

mySpiritRadio